Britain's Future in Europe

CHATHAM HOUSE PAPERS

A West European Programme Publication
Programme Director: Helen Wallace

The Royal Institute of International Affairs, at Chatham House in London, has provided an impartial forum for discussion and debate on current international issues for some 70 years. Its resident research fellows, specialized information resources, and range of publications, conferences, and meetings span the fields of international politics, economics, and security. The Institute is independent of government.

Chatham House Papers are short monographs on current policy problems which have been commissioned by the RIIA. In preparing the papers, authors are advised by a study group of experts convened by the RIIA, and publication of a paper indicates that the Institute regards it as an authoritative contribution to the public debate. The Institute does not, however, hold opinions of its own; the views expressed in this publication are the responsibility of the authors.

CHATHAM HOUSE PAPERS

Britain's Future in Europe

Michael Franklin
with Marc Wilke

The Royal Institute of International Affairs

Pinter Publishers
London

© Royal Institute of International Affairs, 1990

First published in Great Britain in 1990 by
Pinter Publishers Limited
25 Floral Street, London WC2E 9DS

British Library Cataloguing in Publication Data

A CIP catalogue record for this book is available from the British Library

ISBN 0-86187-047-6 (Paperback)
     0-86187-046-8 (Hardback)

Reproduced from copy supplied by
Stephen Austin and Sons Ltd
Printed and bound in Great Britain by
Biddles Ltd

CONTENTS

PREFACE

This study was born out of a concern that Britain might not be getting the best out of its membership of the European Community. I found that concern was shared by many other people, especially during the past year or so when Britain has risked being marginalized, to use an unpleasant term for an unpleasant situation.

I would not have attempted to address this subject without the help and encouragement of many colleagues, both inside and outside Chatham House. The list of acknowledgments is necessarily long, but none the less sincere. Helen Wallace, Director of the West European Programme of the Royal Institute of International Affairs, and William Wallace, the Institute's Deputy Director, have been towers of strength and wise counsellors throughout. Marc Wilke has been my valuable research assistant and provided much of the material for Chapters 8, 9 and 10. His work on the question of subsidiarity has rightly been given wider recognition. The staff of the Institute's Libraries and Publications Department have been unfailingly helpful and always highly professional.

In the Chatham House tradition, I have also drawn on the expertise of a great many people who attended study-group discussions on the various issues addressed in this book. It is not possible to mention them all by name, but I am nevertheless enormously grateful for the time and effort they put into advising me and commenting on various drafts. In addition, I had a number of separate, very helpful, discussions in both London and Brussels. I have to thank Christopher Tugendhat for presiding over many of the discussions and bringing his great experience of the EC to bear. Helen Wallace provided a paper for Chapter 3, David Nicholls and Derek Thomas for Chapter 4, Alan Budd and John Eatwell for Chapter 6, Ann Robinson and Bill Jordan for Chapter 7, Tony Fairclough for Chapter 8, and David Marquand, Carol Tongue, John Biffen and Martyn Bond for Chapter 9. None of these must be expected to accept responsibility for my conclusions or assertions. Barclays, BP and Unilever generously provided funding for this study, together with the Gatsby Charitable Foundation.

Throughout I have used the term British as a matter of convenience, but I have no wish to exclude the citizens of Northern Ireland, who have a keen and particular interest in the future of the EC, of which the Irish Republic is also a member. I have tried to keep the text impersonal, but the final chapter lapses into the use of 'we'. That is deliberate. I wanted to associate myself with the prescriptions which that chapter contains, and especially with any strictures made in it, for which I must carry my share of responsibility.

October 1990   M.F.

1

ENTERING THE 1990s

'A good plot, good friends, and full of expectation;
'An excellent plot, very good friends'
– KING HENRY IV, PT I

When, in July 1990, Jacques Delors, President of the Commission of the European Community (EC), was asked to state the Community's priorities, he said there were no fewer than ten: full realization of the Single European Act (SEA); the Uruguay Round of trade negotiations in the GATT; the two Intergovernmental Conferences (IGCs), on economic and monetary union and on institutional reform;* the summit of the Conference on Security and Cooperation in Europe (CSCE); German unification; relations with Central and Eastern Europe; relations with the European Free Trade Association (EFTA); Mediterranean policy; and the situation in the Soviet Union. Each of these topics raises important issues which will affect the EC in the 1990s and its relationships with the rest of the world.

A few weeks later he would doubtless have added the crisis brought about by the Iraqi invasion, on 2 August, of Kuwait. It remains to be seen whether the Community's initial disarray over this crisis will weaken its influence or goad it into more effective procedures for the future. Either way, the Community faces a

* These two Intergovernmental Conferences are scheduled to run in parallel, beginning in December 1990. Representatives of all the EC governments will be negotiating amendments to the Treaties, which will subsequently have to be ratified by the national parliaments.

formidable agenda. Partly through its own efforts and partly through the force of circumstances it has both achieved greatness and had greatness thrust upon it. At the start of the 1990s, for the first time in its history, the EC looks like becoming the third economic force in the world alongside the United States and Japan, and a potential third political force alongside the two superpowers.

At the beginning of the 1980s such a claim would have seemed incredible. The EC appeared to be stagnating. Britain was preoccupied with the start of the Thatcher revolution, and France with the ill-fated experiment of socialism in one country. In Germany, the *Ostpolitik* lay dormant. Unemployment was high in all EC countries, and the protectionist pressures to which this gave rise were barely contained. The internal agenda was dominated by squabbles over the Community budget and worries about how to accommodate Spain and Portugal. The European Parliament remained a frustrated and largely ineffective talking-shop. Elsewhere in Western Europe, nothing much was happening either, for there was little movement in EFTA. Further to the East, the iron curtain seemed to represent a permanent divide. NATO had a clearly defined role and, for all that it had its headquarters in the same city, went its way without reference to the EC.

By the mid-1980s, for a number of reasons, the climate of opinion began to change. Industry, concerned at the technological lag in Europe and rising competition from the newly industrialized countries, called for a concerted European response and a stronger and more cohesive internal market. Governments, concerned at the vacillations in American defence, foreign, trade and exchange-rate policies, felt that Europe should strengthen itself. The Community institutions, concerned at the problems of enlarging the Community from nine to twelve, wanted better decision-making procedures.

All this came together in 1985: the Community had put behind it nagging problems like the British budget contribution; a new, stronger Commission arrived; the decision was taken to have a Treaty-amending conference; and a programme was drawn up and endorsed to achieve a genuine common market by the end of 1992. The whole Community was galvanized and gave birth to the Single European Act, which not only produced the legal muscle to make the 1992 target possible but gave greater powers to the European Parliament, brought environment and technology within the ambit of the Treaties, gave status to the separate foreign policy procedures and introduced into the EC the notion of its economic and social cohesion. The SEA represented a significant transfer of powers to the Community and another important step in the gradual drawing together of the member states as foreseen by the Community's founding fathers.

These stirrings within the Community led the EFTA countries to re-examine their relationships with the EC and to wonder whether they might not be better inside. Further afield, the United States and Japan came to deal increasingly (though not exclusively) with the EC as an economic and political entity. The Commission was given a seat at the table of the economic summit meetings. Economic relations with the Community assumed increasing importance, even if they were not always easy. The very success of the Community provoked exaggerated fears abroad, notably in the USA, that the EC would turn itself into a Fortress Europe, stifling external competition as it opened up competition within its borders. This was but one of the factors persuading the world that another round of trade negotiations would be desirable. At the heart of the decision in 1986 to launch the so-called Uruguay Round was the realization by governments that the world's economies (like those of the EC) were becoming more and more interdependent as a result of the links created by technology, the multinationals and the free movement of capital.

Once the 1992 programme was on its way, the EC turned its attention to other longstanding sores, such as the Common Agricultural Policy (CAP) and the inequities and inadequacies of the Community's budgetary system. Skilful negotiation saw some resolution of these matters (though they will recur) in a successful package deal in 1988. By the beginning of 1989, the Community was riding high.

Flushed with these successes and eager for more, the Commission – encouraged by the European Parliament and most of the member states – began to plan the next leap forward. This was to be no less than economic and monetary union (EMU) and what were rapidly seen as the necessary accompanying steps towards political union.

In the midst of all this activity came Gorbachev and the revolutions in Eastern Europe. Europe entered the maelstrom. As one country after another overthrew its communist dictatorship, the newly democratized governments looked to the West for help. East Germany, thought at the time by most people to be the probable back marker, overtook them all and became part of a unified Germany less than one year from the pulling down of the Berlin Wall. While Europe was still struggling to understand the implications of what was happening in the East, Iraq invaded Kuwait, opening up a security threat to the south instead of to the east.

Faced with these dramatic changes, it is impossible to discern what will be the pattern of the 1990s. The rapidity with which the scene has shifted has brought, to borrow George Robertson's phrase, a 'bonfire of the certainties'. No one knows whether the changes in the Soviet Union are irreversible or how successful it will be in consolidating democracy and improving living standards. The same question-marks must hang to a greater or lesser extent over the countries of Central and Eastern Europe. The Middle East has been plunged into conflict. Could the world find itself in recession as a result of another oil crisis or a breakdown in the world trading system? Any or all of these changes would alter the framework within which the EC must work out its own destiny.

Britain is an important member of the EC, but it has never played the leadership role which many people hoped and expected that it would. Although in recent years it has had some major successes, notably in promoting the drive towards a single market, its influence within the Community has not prospered and its relations with other EC countries have often been uncomfortable. There have even been times when its views were apparently ignored by its Community partners. The principal aim of this study is to throw light on why this should be so and to suggest ways in which Britain can play a more constructive and influential role. The scene having been set in this introductory chapter, Chapter 2 moves on to examine why Britain has been seen as a reluctant partner and often finds itself isolated. The subsequent chapters look at its role in the fundamental choices and tasks which are now facing the Community. First of these is whether the EC should extend its membership further and how this might best be done. This is dealt with in Chapter 3. Chapter 4 extends the discussion about the EC's relations with its neighbours to look at the scope of its activities and in particular its involvement with foreign, defence and security policies. The following three chapters deal with the major issues on the economic agenda, and particularly EMU (Chapter 6), and try to discern British interest in each area and how that can best be furthered. Chapter 8 deals with environmental policy. Chapters 9 and 10 address the political and institutional issues as seen in Britain and elsewhere in the Community. A final chapter offers suggestions as to how Britain might take its rightful place in the Community and play an effective role in its future development.

The postwar face of Europe changed in the space of months. The cold war has been officially declared over. Germany has been united. The pace of change has left people and governments breathless and confused. Some have reacted more quickly and effectively than others. The Commission was quick off the mark, welcoming the prospect of German unification and coping well with the invitation from the Paris summit to lead the Western response to requests for assistance from Eastern Europe. But it has shown a strong tendency to want to steam ahead on internal integration without enough thought for the consequences of these dramatic new developments. Germany, at the centre of events, moved rapidly into a leadership role. Anxious to assure its EC partners that the new *Ostpolitik* posed no threat to either its EC or its NATO membership, the West German government readily fell in with the view that events called for a strengthening of the Community and no slackening in the pace of closer integration. Even so, it was inevitable that others in the Community should be fearful at the prospect of a united Germany and the danger of a resurgent nationalism. Nowhere was this more so than in France, where the government rapidly reached the conclusion that it, too, wanted a 'European Germany and not a German Europe' (an expression first used by the former German Chancellor, Helmut Schmidt). Thus the two dominant EC players were agreed that the correct response was a tighter Community and, in particular, a European monetary system (EMS) rather than a Deutschmark zone.

Britain shared these worries over German unification but, in the rush of events, allowed prejudice to rule over judgment. Germans were upset when British ministers expressed their fears too publicly. Recovery was swift but not before serious damage was done to relations. At the same time, the British Prime Minister was making it clear that she did not share the enthusiasm of the rest of the Community for greater economic and political integration. Thus

Britain was wrong-footed in its reactions to events in Germany and alone in assessing the consequences for the EC. It did not appear to have any alternative strategy to the one chosen by its Community partners. For a time it was a case of fog in Britain and Britain isolated.

2
BRITAIN THE RELUCTANT PARTNER

'Hath Britain all the sun that shines?'
– CYMBELINE

To understand why Britain found itself in such an uncomfortable position at the beginning of 1990, some brief historical background is needed. When Britain at last succeeded in entering the EC in 1973, there was no way in which postwar history could be unwritten. The British carried a legacy with them. The Churchillian euphoria about a 'United States of Europe' in the early postwar years had not borne fruit in any readiness on Britain's part to join with the original Six when they created first the European Coal and Steel Community and then the EEC and Euratom. Indeed the British government had done worse than stand aside. It had sought – through Reginald Maudling's plan in 1958 for a free-trade area – to have the commercial advantages without taking any of the political responsibilities. By the early 1960s, the Continental perception of Britain as the 'reluctant partner' was already firmly established.

When in 1961 the government of Harold Macmillan at last applied to join, it seemed to many on the Continent that, while necessity and the realization that the enterprise was actually going to work had convinced the British, their hearts were not in it. Although the remaining Five were upset by de Gaulle's veto and did their best to override it, some of them had a sneaking feeling that he was not entirely wrong in thinking that Britain was not ready. By the time it did join, much had been settled (notably the Common Agricultural

Policy) which was uncongenial to Britain; conversely, Britain carried into the Community commitments (notably to New Zealand) which were uncongenial to its partners. Although parliament was persuaded to pass the necessary legislation, a strong anti-European faction existed on both sides of the House, and when a Labour government was returned to power it forced a renegotiation of the terms of entry and a subsequent referendum. Although that endorsed Britain's membership, public opinion remained notably less enthusiastic than elsewhere in the EC.[1]

British accession coincided with the first oil crisis. Although North Sea oil was only beginning to come on stream, there was an opportunity for Britain to show some solidarity with its new-found partners. Instead, the Heath government adopted a very nationalistic posture, which got things off to a bad start. Then came the Labour government's decision to renegotiate the terms of entry, which was inevitably unsettling despite the subsequent favourable endorsement in the referendum. Moreover, renegotiation had not disposed of the problem of Britain's inequitable contribution to the Community budget. It could no longer be swept under the carpet, and the attempt to put it right proved to be a highly divisive issue for several years. Resolved provisionally in May 1980, and definitively in 1984, it did much to perpetuate a sense of 'them and us' both in Brussels and among the public in Britain. It was doubly unfortunate that the issue came to a head at the start of a Conservative administration which otherwise seemed destined to adopt a more constructive attitude, and that it fell to be dealt with by a Prime Minister who enjoys a fight. While the outcome was very satisfactory (for Britain, but also for the whole Community), and could not have been secured without very tough negotiating, the bruises left by the battle have had their effect more generally on Britain's relations with other EC members. Just as importantly, it developed in the British government a confrontational mentality towards the Community which ministers have found hard to throw off.[2]

The Atlantic connection

Much of the explanation for Britain's uneasy relationship with the rest of the EC can be found either in the issue of sovereignty (discussed below) or in the pull of the Atlantic connection. During the early postwar period, the majority of the British people gave priority to the ties with the Commonwealth and with the United States. As the historical and trade links with the Commonwealth weakened, so it diminished as a factor in British policy. But for reasons of language and popular culture, shared war experience and continuing strategic interest, many British people, particularly of the older generation, still relate more readily to America than to the rest of Europe. Indeed, it was only during the 1980s that the British appeared to accept that they were European as well as British (or English, Scottish or Welsh). At government level, the consciousness of America's strategic importance as an ally and partner has caused successive governments to seek to sustain the 'special relationship' between Britain and the United States. Time and again – from Prime Minister Harold Macmillan's controversial nuclear deal with President Kennedy in 1962, just at a critical point in the negotiations for EC entry, to British instinctive support for the American line in the Iraqi conflict in 1990 – reaction at the highest levels has almost always been an Atlanticist rather than a European one. Among ministers and officials, divisions have grown up between 'Atlanticists', often involved with security-related issues, and 'Europeans' concerned more with economic issues.

The balance has undoubtedly shifted as successive American administrations have made it clear that they favour closer European integration and British participation in it. Moreover, the significance of the 'special relationship' has waned as the Americans have progressively strengthened their ties with other European countries, and above all with Germany. Nevertheless the pull of the English-speaking relationship remains a strong thread running through Britain's external relations and exerts an influence, though a declining one, on attitudes to Europe not found elsewhere in the EC. But it is not as significant as the question of sovereignty.

Sovereignty: the misunderstood obsession

Whereas the prevalent attitude of the British people towards the EC in general is one of indifference, there is a strong streak of antagonism, deriving from the sense of loss of national sovereignty, to the supranational institutions of the Community. No amount of explanation that there is nothing new in the sharing of sovereignty with other countries has removed the feeling that national control has been lost. No amount of recognition that the watershed was

9

passed when Britain formally joined the Community has reconciled some people to the past. It has made them only more determined to resist further erosion. No amount of ridicule at the fact that the British are clinging to the shadow of sovereignty (e.g. over exchange rates) when economic realities leave them with no option has changed political attitudes, at least in some quarters. No attempt to differentiate the question of sovereignty from that of national or cultural identity has so far been successful in dispelling the myth that a further pooling of sovereignty in the EC will mean the suppression of the British way of life with all its distinctiveness.

As has often been explained,[3] the reason for this apparent perversity is largely to be found in the identification of sovereignty with the peculiarly British institution of an all-powerful national parliament, subject, for all practical purposes, to no constitutional limitations and able to delegate powers to lower levels of government or not as it thinks fit. Thus a loss of power from the Westminster parliament is seen as a loss of national power. And since Westminster MPs are the most directly affected, it is they who tend to be the most resistant to transfers of responsibility to the Community institutions. Moreover, political power in Britain has traditionally been considered to be indivisible, belonging to the government of the day and not to be shared with anyone else. Policy is changed when the government changes and another party takes over on the all-or-nothing parliamentary system. Thus 'Britain's political culture remains unusually – perhaps uniquely – unfavourable ... to the kind of power-sharing implied by membership of the European Community'.[4]

The situation among Continental countries is quite different. In the first place, none of them has had the centuries of uninterrupted constitutional stability of Britain. Whether through war or political upheaval, their political systems are of comparatively recent date. Thus they neither carry the same accretion of myth nor are they all felt to have unique virtue. Secondly, in all the major Continental countries, the political system is much more a consensual one, based on alliances and compromise with no winner-takes-all. And, thirdly, whether through a federal system, as in Germany, or through conscious political choice, as in Italy and Spain, power is shared between the centre and the regions. Thus the concepts of power-sharing and consensual politics, which characterize the EC, are familiar and not alien. The British obsession with sovereignty is neither shared nor understood elsewhere in the EC (or, indeed, in all parts of the United Kingdom: it is an English, not a Scottish perception). Even the Danes, who have until recently shared many of these preoccupations, have now made a conscious political decision to rally to the majority position (see Chapter 10).

Even in Britain, attitudes are shifting. There is a body of opinion which, apart from the EC implications, now questions the traditional lack of a written constitution in which some rights other than those of the Westminster parliament might become entrenched. The virtue of a system which divides power between the Community, the nation and the region is not lost on the Scots, whose case for greater autonomy has so far foundered on the invincible power of Westminster. More and more people are realizing that economic interdependence and the open economy (fostered by the same strain of Thatcherism which takes a politically nationalistic view) have undermined the scope for independent national action, sovereignty's *raison d'être*. Thus the traditional British attitudes caricatured at the beginning of this section are on the wane, but they are still widespread, and strongly held and expressed by a determined minority.

A Thatcherite view of Europe

The most striking expression of this minority view came in Mrs Thatcher's Bruges speech of September 1988 and more recently in her speech to the Aspen Institute, Colorado, in August 1990. The latter contained a strong endorsement of the Atlantic connection. Both sought to call a halt to further integration involving the transfer of national sovereignty to Community institutions, especially in the field of economic and monetary policy (see Chapter 6). In part this attitude is based on the belief that the exercise of power at Community level necessarily means more government, whereas Thatcherism is dedicated to less intervention. But it also derives from the strong nationalistic streak in Mrs Thatcher's approach.

In this respect, it is a fundamentally Gaullist view of Europe, based on 'the willing cooperation between independent sovereign states',[5] rather than the integrationist approach now favoured by most of the rest of the Community, including the French. It seeks to perpetuate a dichotomy which has existed ever since Britain joined the EC, 'pretending that General de Gaulle's version of Europe, cooperation between wholly sovereign states, had won the day, whereas in truth it had failed to break the Community mechanism and the process of integration was picking up speed again'.[6]

Such an attitude has resurfaced at each turning-point in the Community and became particularly apparent when the EC came to discuss its reactions to events in Eastern Europe. The Prime Minister appeared to want to call a halt to the process of integration within the Community so as not to make it harder for those East Europeans who saw membership of the EC as their eventual goal. The remainder of the Community, led by France, Germany and the Commission, decided rapidly and decisively that, far from slackening the pace, events in East Germany and Eastern Europe in general called for an acceleration of the integration process. Britain had no option but to acquiesce. But the sense of frustration with Britain's attitude became very apparent, and the sense of isolation referred to at the end of the previous chapter was real. Since that time, the British government has made efforts to get back into the game, and the rest of the Community has evidently decided that it has no wish to isolate Britain unless Britain isolates itself.

At this point it is worth asking why, in government circles, Britain has such a bad reputation with the rest of the Community when in the practical running of EC affairs it is acknowledged that the British perform very creditably and have indeeed, in several important areas, been in the lead. In particular, the Thatcher government has throughout shown great enthusiasm and provided a great deal of the impulse in ideas and practice relating to the 1992 programme – the biggest single item on the Community's agenda in the second half of the 1980s. It has been constructive and supportive of most of the Commission's proposals. Not only did it accept the substantial increase in majority voting provided for in the SEA, but it has played the majority-voting game with skill and without any public outcry. Its record in implementing the 1992 decisions has been exemplary. Nor is this critical attitude in government circles found in other quarters. Among the business community, and in institutions like the Economic and Social Committee, British participation is well respected and valued.

Why, then, is Britain still regarded as such an awkward partner? Part of the answer lies in style. The confrontational habit bred during the budget battle dies hard. When we do have a good record, as with the implementation of the 1992 programme, we tend to sound self-righteous. But a large part of the answer lies in the attempt to reconcile a liberal, free-market economic philosophy with a strongly nationalistic political vision of Europe.[7] Bringing down the frontiers between the member states and allowing the free movement of goods, capital, services and people appeared to be fully consistent with the Thatcherite goals. But then came the fear that acting on the European stage would compromise or even suppress some of the purity of free-market principles as applied in Britain.

The impression has been created that, given the choice, the British would rather preserve the purity of their own system than achieve a lesser degree of liberalization but on a European scale. The conflict became even more acute when it touched on the central levers of national power, such as fiscal harmonization, border controls or fixed exchange rates. Yes to a single market, but no to a single currency. The rest of the Community perceives that Britain is prepared to go thus far and no further.

Changing perceptions

It is clear that there are elements within the government who are disturbed by the risk of British isolation and determined to prevent it happening. In this they have the support of the majority of Conservative MPs, although it is clear that there is a powerful minority who share Mrs Thatcher's views.[8] Conservative Members of the European Parliament (MEPs) are pressing the government to go much further in support of mainstream European thinking, and many now openly espouse federalist views which until recently have been articulated only by Liberals. It is not clear how these tensions within the Conservative Party will be resolved, but the evidence that public opinion – and, even more decisively, business opinion – has now become much more open to the European argument is bound to have a significant effect.

Although inevitably influenced by domestic, i.e. non-EC, factors, the European elections of 1989 are widely thought to have marked a shift in British public attitudes towards the EC and away from the confrontational approach which has marked so much of the government's dealings in Brussels. Opinion polls bear this out. As Table 1 shows, between 1973 and 1989 the proportion of the public that regarded the EC as 'a good thing' (which dipped to a very low figure in 1981 at the height of the battle over the British budget contribution) rose significantly. No doubt the perceived success of the '1992' process, and Britain's part in it, was a contributory factor.

Table 1   Shifting attitudes and interests

	Percentage of total UK international trade (exports plus imports) with other EC countries	Percentage of UK population thinking EC a good thing
1973	36	31*
1977	41	35
1981	45	26
1985	49	38
1989	52	50

Sources: Department of Trade and Industry; EC Commission, *Eurobarometer: Public Opinion in the EC, Evolution 1974–1989*, vol. II, no. 32 (December 1989).
*Excluding Northern Ireland.

Other evidence suggests that support for greater integration is also growing. In a poll carried out by Gallup for the EC Commission in April 1989,[9] 70% of British people were in favour of unification, up from 61% the previous autumn. However, a more accurate impression of attitudes is probably given by the replies to more specific questions asked in a poll conducted by Gallup for the *Daily Telegraph* a few months later:[10] 13% favoured a fully integrated Europe, with most major decisions being taken by a European government; 48% favoured a Europe more integrated than now, but with decisions that primarily affected Britain staying in British hands; 21% preferred the situation much as it is now, with Britain retaining a veto over major policy changes that it does not like; 12% wanted British withdrawal; and 7% registered don't knows. There is little doubt that the degree of support for further integration would have been significantly lower in earlier years. The British public no longer automatically assumes that the government is always right and Brussels always wrong.

This shift in public opinion has been accompanied, and doubtless influenced, by the now strongly expressed view of business. British business has for some time been generally positive about the EC: in June 1989 no less than 94% of business people questioned thought it 'a good thing'.[11] In part this can be explained by the extent to which trade is now focused on the EC. The key statistics appear in Table 1. They have been put alongside the figures for public attitudes, not to suggest any causal relationship, but because the coincidence of trends is interesting.

Whereas when Britain joined the EC many people in British industry were sceptical about the alleged 'dynamic' effects of entry on the country's economic performance, in recent years British business has become more confident of its ability to compete. This is especially true of the financial sector, which now accounts for a larger share of the British economy, is acknowledged to have comparative advantage in Europe and could stand to gain considerably from the liberalization of financial services envisaged under the 1992 programme.[12] Indeed, the unilateral opening-up of the economy under the free-market policies of the Thatcher government left British business with little alternative but to see the EC as its market-place. The strong pressure from British industry for a 'level playing-field' in Europe is a reflection of the same phenomenon. Finally, the preoccupation with political sovereignty has not been shared by the business community. Its essential interest lies in the practical merits of further integration.

Perhaps the most significant change in attitude has occurred on the left of British politics. Although the Labour Party remains cautious about further integration and shares the views of Mrs Thatcher about the importance of widening the EC to embrace Eastern Europe, it has given up its traditional anti-European stance. In part this followed an earlier policy shift by the leadership of the Trades Union Congress, which saw that its members might be better served under a European social policy than under a national government with strong free-market convictions; and in part it reflected a recognition by left-wing intellectuals that, as the French discovered in 1981–2, economic interdependence now made it almost impossible to pursue socialist policies in one country alone. These perceptions found expression in the Labour Party manifesto for the 1989 elections to the European Parliament, where it was able to cite cases in which EC proposals would have brought greater benefits to the voter than those available under national law. This change of attitude has enabled the Labour Party to criticize the government for not being sufficiently active and effective in Brussels. While supportive of British entry into the exchange-rate mechanism (ERM), the Labour Party's attitude to economic and monetary union is probably not far from that of the government. As with the Conservative Party, Labour's MEPs are now mainly ahead of the

Party in their support for further integration in Europe, and one of their number, David Martin, has been the rapporteur for two reports of the European Parliament which go further than official Labour Party policy.

Thus, although the earlier period of apparent hostility across most of the political spectrum undoubtedly contributed to Britain's lack of influence and credibility within the Community, the rest of the Community can at least now see political circumstances in which a more positive stance on the part of British government could emerge. As the following chapters will show, there are major issues on the EC agenda where British views and experience are highly relevant. It is important not only for Britain but for the Community as a whole that this potentially constructive influence should be effectively brought to bear.

Britain no longer deserves the charge of being a reluctant partner. Hesitant would be the more appropriate term. What is needed now is a jump from hesitancy to commitment.

3

THE MAGNETIC PULL OF
THE EC

'Let me not to the marriage of true minds
'Admit impediment'
– SONNET 117

The stated position of the Community is that no further enlargement is possible until the completion of the single market at the end of 1992. This has not prevented a queue of potential members from forming. This chapter examines some of the options open to the Community in responding to these overtures and identifies Britain's position on the issue.

It was back in 1987 that Turkey tabled its application for membership, even if everyone knew at the time that, given the political and economic problems, its incorporation into the EC would be far from quick or easy – if indeed it can happen at all. In July 1989 Austria applied, presenting none of the problems that Turkey did, but was firmly told that nothing was possible before 1993. Malta and Cyprus have also tabled applications. All the new democracies of Central and Eastern Europe have said that membership of the EC is their eventual aim. Czechoslovakia and Hungary are probably in the greatest hurry, and recently the Prime Ministers of Austria and Hungary declared jointly that their common aim is for their countries to become members once the single market is completed. Among the Scandinavian countries, Norway is hesitating to renew the application which lapsed in 1972, Sweden is again warming to the idea of membership, the new political alignment of Europe makes Finnish membership no longer unthinkable and even

Iceland is 'beginning to contemplate the unpalatable consequences of being the only European member of NATO which is outside the EC'.[1] Decisions for these countries, as for Switzerland, will await the negotiations on a European Economic Area discussed below.

As Figure 1 illustrates, all these potential members form a ring around the existing Community to the north, the east and the south. But they present a motley picture. Figure 1 shows that they range in size from Turkey, with a population equal to that of Britain or France (and growing fast), to Malta and Iceland, which are no bigger than Luxembourg. The differences in terms of wealth are just as striking.

Table 2 takes the figures for population and GDP (with some adjustments for Eastern Europe) and expresses them in terms of wealth per head. The ranking order is remarkable. Whereas the EFTA countries are actually wealthier than the existing EC, the countries of Eastern Europe all have a GDP per head way below the EC average, roughly comparable with those of Greece and Portugal. Turkey's income per head is scarcely one-tenth the EC average. Behind these figures lie, on the one hand, economies which already trade heavily with the EC and are well adapted to the competitive and sophisticated EC market and, on the other hand, those which have had very little economic interchange with the West for 40 years and are only just emerging from the rigidities and inefficiencies of central planning. It is therefore impossible to treat the applicants or potential applicants as a group.

EFTA and the European Economic Area
The driving force for most of the EFTA countries is the fear of being excluded from the EC market and the wish to share in the benefits of 1992. Political considerations have been secondary, though this is changing as the EC becomes involved in issues like assistance to the emerging democracies of Central and Eastern Europe, where EFTA countries have a keen interest. Although Austria has felt obliged to express a reservation about its neutral status, its anxiety to join means that it would be willing to sign up to the *acquis communautaire* almost without condition. At the other end of the spectrum, most Swiss still want to retain their independence. However, attitudes are changing with the recognition that it may in the end prove difficult to secure the benefits of economic integration without the political commitment of membership.

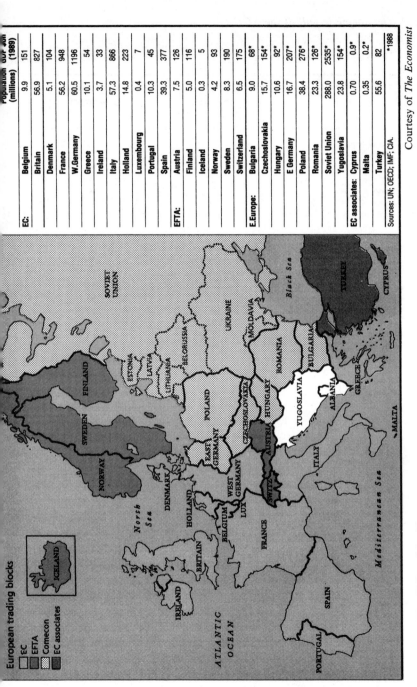

European trading blocks	Population (millions)	GDP $ bn (1989)
EC:		
Belgium	9.9	151
Britain	56.9	827
Denmark	5.1	104
France	56.2	948
W.Germany	60.5	1196
Greece	10.1	54
Ireland	3.7	33
Italy	57.3	866
Holland	14.8	223
Luxembourg	0.4	7
Portugal	10.3	45
Spain	39.3	377
EFTA:		
Austria	7.5	126
Finland	5.0	116
Iceland	0.3	5
Norway	4.2	93
Sweden	8.3	190
Switzerland	6.5	175
E.Europe:		
Bulgaria	9.0	68*
Czechoslovakia	15.7	154*
Hungary	10.6	92*
E Germany	16.7	207*
Poland	38.4	276*
Romania	23.3	126*
Soviet Union	288.0	2535*
Yugoslavia	23.8	154*
EC associates: Cyprus	0.70	0.9*
Malta	0.35	0.2*
Turkey	55.6	82

Sources: UN; OECD; IMF; CIA.   *1988

Courtesy of *The Economist*

Figure 1   The EC and its European partners

Table 2   For richer, for poorer

	Index of GDP per head EC average = 100*	Population (millions)
The very rich (EFTA)		
Switzerland	182	6
Finland	157	5
Sweden	155	8
Norway	150	4
Austria	114	7
The mostly rich (EC)		
Denmark	138	5
Germany**	123 (118)	77
Luxembourg	118	0.4
France	114	56
Belgium	103	10
Italy	102	57
Netherlands	102	15
UK	98	57
Spain	65	39
Ireland	60	4
Greece	36	10
Portugal	31	10
The not-so-rich (Eastern Europe)		
Czechoslovakia	51	16
Hungary	44	11
Bulgaria	38	9
Poland	37	38
Romania	28	23
The poor		
Turkey	9	56

Source: *The Economist*, 7 July 1990.
*Including the former GDR.
**The figure in parentheses is based on lower estimates of GDP in the former GDR (see, for example, J. Rollo, *The New Eastern Europe: Western Responses*, RIIA/Pinter, 1990).

It was to respond to these wishes and at the same time to put off the issue of membership that in January 1989 the Commission resurrected the 1984 Declaration which pledged the EC and EFTA together to create a European Economic Space, or European Economic Area (EEA) as it is now to be called. Negotiations during 1990 are designed to establish whether it is possible to create a privileged partnership which would extend the single market (but not the CAP or the common commercial policy) to EFTA without requiring the EFTA countries to join the EC. The crux of the negotiations is how much say EFTA can have in the decisions of the EC and how the EC can be sure that its disciplines, e.g. on competition policy and state aids, are applied in the EFTA countries.

These difficult issues were not made any easier by the Commission's unwillingness to substantiate an earlier offer that EFTA would have some share in the Community's decision-making processes – somewhat surprising given the Commission's evident interest in a successful outcome as a means to postpone any decisions on enlargement. If the negotiations fail, it is obvious that Austria will pursue its preferred solution of full membership and perhaps be joined by others; but the problem for the EC will not go away. If the negotiations succeed, they will provide a convenient solution to the EC's relations with its economically closest counterparts, either on a permanent basis or, as they are increasingly seen by both sides, as an interim process in the approach of EFTA countries to eventual full membership. Either way, they will be closely studied for the lessons to be drawn for other potential applicants. Israel, for one, would like to make a similar arrangement.

Helping the new democracies

When in the mid-1970s the newly democratic governments of Spain and Portugal applied for EC membership (as Greece had done earlier, following the departure of the Colonels), the EC members bit the bullet and agreed to welcome them in spite of their economic backwardness. In the event, the absorption of Spain and Portugal into the EC has gone a great deal more smoothly than most people expected. Now the Community is faced with a similar and even bigger challenge. For historical reasons, which William Wallace has recently analysed,[2] and because they are seeking to remodel their economies on market lines, the countries of Central and Eastern Europe are inevitably looking to EC membership as their goal. As Wallace says:

> The evident prosperity and technical advance of Western
> Europe have pulled the countries of Eastern Europe westwards.
> The combination of political stability, limited government,
> social partnership and economic success has provided a West
> European model to which intellectuals and dissidents in Eastern
> Europe have referred, in evident contrast to the failures of the
> East European order ... The new governments of Eastern
> Europe are asserting their determination to 'rejoin the West'
> more than to design some new pan-European order.

The absorption of East Germany into the EC by virtue of German reunification can only have added another spur to that determination. It is probably too early to judge whether joining the EC as it is, and as it is likely to become, represents a definitive view of the long-run ambitions or interests of the new governments, but it appears to epitomize their current aspirations. They are moving in uncharted waters and so to an extent is the Community.

How should the EC respond? It has every reason to encourage the establishment of stable and prosperous democracies among its eastern neighbours. It is thus as unthinkable to rebuff the aspirations of those East European countries which have now chosen democracy as it was in the cases of Greece, Spain and Portugal. But the problems are formidable. The new democratic institutions are in their infancy. Their existing economic links with the West are slender. Their economies are in a parlous state, and in the short run the necessary changes in economic management can only add to the tensions. To quote a recent study:

> The combination of short-term macroeconomic problems, the
> need for long-term systemic reform and the impact of
> democracy on the expectations of the people will be hard to
> manage. The only sure predictions are that the process will take
> time and that mistakes will be made – both in the reforming
> countries and by those trying to help from outside.[3]

It is quite clear that the immediate need in Eastern Europe is for economic aid and, as described in the next chapter, the EC is in the forefront of the effort now being made, beginning with the newly created European Bank for Reconstruction and Development. It will be some time before the full extent of the help needed is known.

But it is likely to be massive. The Community will need to make a very careful assessment of how much it is able and prepared to do in relation to what others can be expected to contribute and to the claims made upon it from other quarters. It cannot have escaped the notice of the countries of Eastern Europe – as it should not be forgotten by those who support their entry – that they are bound to have a greater claim on the Community budget as potential or actual members than would be the case if they were outside.

For the time being, Eastern Europe needs an arm's-length relationship with the EC, but a friendly arm which assists with know-how, management skills and investment. The Commission has proposed the negotiation of Association Agreements which provide a flexible relationship with the EC but contain no reference to possible membership. Poland, Hungary and Czechoslovakia are likely to be the first countries to be involved in negotiations on this basis. As conceived by the British Foreign and Commonwealth Office, which has played a large part in devising them, the form and content of Association Agreements can evolve as political and economic reforms take root: providing a bridge to membership if things go well or, if the reform process runs off the rails, the possibility of pulling back.

But it is doubtful whether this approach will be sufficient to satisfy the political aspirations of the new governments. It is clear that any idea of a link-up with EFTA as a half-way house to EC membership holds no appeal either for the EFTA countries or for the countries of Eastern Europe. Both have their eyes set on the EC. The solution is not easy to see, but the obligation towards Eastern Europe is clear. The EC was created as a means of reconciliation between France and Germany: the economic provisions were a means and not an end in themselves. The need again is for reconciliation between countries which have been divided for 40 years by the iron curtain. The EC should not allow its own economic or political preoccupations to stand in the way of an imaginative response.

The southern flank
In its dealings with the rest of the Mediterranean area, the EC has not distinguished itself. In spite of the fact that all countries round the Mediterranean are overwhelmingly dependent on the EC economically, most commercial negotiations have produced meagre

results in terms of access for Mediterranean products into the Community. The European textile interests and the protective clauses of the CAP have seen to that. The Mediterranean countries now face the prospect of competing in the EC with the East Europeans, who themselves will be wanting to provide agricultural products, textiles and the kind of manufactured goods which North Africa will have to develop, not to mention labour.

It was more out of a sense of frustration than any serious hope of success that Morocco applied for membership in 1987. If for no other reason than fear of mass immigration from the burgeoning population of North Africa (see Chapter 7), the EC is going to have to take much more seriously the claims of its southern neighbours to a place in the economic sun. The Commission is seeking the adoption of a multi-pronged strategy: Community aid to finance economic cooperation, environmental protection and training; the promotion of joint ventures and private enterprise; better market access for non-EC Mediterranean products; and more technical help to foster better domestic commercial opportunities. The emphasis is heavily on aid rather than trade. The Commission has strong support from Italy and other EC countries of the south, which want to concentrate on the aid aspects so as not to engender too much opposition from the farm sector on the question of access for agricultural products. Britain and other northern member states, on the other hand, object to the financial commitment involved and will press for more to be done on access. The fact of the matter is that both will be needed.

Most conscious of this need are those closest geographically, Spain and Italy. They take the first shock of illegal immigration, and it is the agriculture of southern Europe which is most at risk from North African competition. On the other hand, Spain and Italy see political advantage in promoting closer ties with the rest of the Mediterranean and even the accession of the Mediterranean islands as a means of strengthening the already powerful Mediterranean group within the EC. But Italian aspirations within the Community have never been limited to the southern flank. Mention should be made of its attempts to foster the creation of a 'Pentagonale', a grouping reminiscent of the old Austro-Hungarian empire and consisting of Italy, Austria, Hungary, Czechoslovakia and Yugoslavia. Conceived as a way of helping the newly democratized members – among which Italy has rapidly growing commercial interests – to develop, it may possibly create an additional source of pressure for earlier rather than later membership.

Turkey is a special case. A member of NATO and the OECD, it has pride of place in the queue. Even if its strategic importance as the guardian of NATO's southern flank is now diminished, it may not have disappeared. And as its role in the economic blockade of Iraq has amply demonstrated, its strategic position remains of great importance to Europe and the West, a buffer between Europe and the Islamic fundamentalism and instability of the Middle East. It is for these reasons that no one in the Community has been bold enough to say that Turkey is not part of Europe and therefore does not qualify for membership.[4] It is equally clear that the Community sees tremendous problems in accommodating Turkey, not only because of its burgeoning population[5] and primitive economy but because of the quarrel with Greece over Cyprus (another potential member).

Where does the Community go from here?

Opinion in Britain, as in many parts of the Community, remains fundamentally ambivalent about enlargement, recognizing the case for it but not wishing to face up to the consequences – either that the Community will have to become more supranational in order to cope with a larger and even more diverse membership or that, if it fails to do so, it will become ineffective and slow-moving. The potential conflict between 'widening' the Community to include others and 'deepening' its internal functioning has long troubled EC policy-makers.[6] As noted in Chapter 2, the debate surfaced again in the wake of events in Eastern Europe, when Britain stood alone against 'deepening', but was rapidly resolved by the rest of the Community in favour of pressing on with plans for further integration, and notably with EMU, irrespective of the possible consequences elsewhere in Europe. France in particular was convinced that the best way to prevent a renascent German nationalism and to control the financial power of the Deutschmark was to harness it to the EC machine. Other member states felt strongly that the Community needed to be more cohesive in order to fulfil its role in Europe – strong in order to be generous, as Delors put it. But he and others in the Community went further, arguing that, at least for the

25

foreseeable future, the Community should repel boarders and concentrate on its internal programme.

In Britain, there are those who take the diametrically opposite point of view, supporting further enlargement precisely because, besides being desirable in itself, it is likely in their opinion to lead to a looser form of association within the Community and slow down the process of integration. Advocates of this view (discussed further in Chapter 10) would deny using enlargement of the Community as a form of sabotage; but the suspicion of British motives in Community circles is such that any advocacy of enlargement, whether from those who favour European integration or from those who are opposed to it, tends to be discounted.

No doubt, as Helen Wallace argues in her excellent summary of the issues at stake, 'the optimal choice for the EC, now as on previous occasions, should be both to consolidate, i.e. complete and deepen, and to build open-ended partnerships, which could test the ground for subsequent enlargement'.[7] What might these 'open-ended partnerships' be? In the case of EFTA, the negotiations for a European Economic Area are clearly designed to fit that bill, and, in spite of the obstacles discussed earlier, it is very much to be hoped that they will succeed. If they do, they might possibly provide a way of dealing with other minor candidates. But it is not the solution for Eastern Europe or for Turkey. For these countries, more serious thought should be given to some form of two-tier Community, or in another formulation, a Europe of concentric circles.[8]

In either formulation, there would be an inner core of EC member countries more closely integrated than the second tier or circle, which might include existing EC members, EFTA countries and other potential applicants. The rest of Europe would constitute the third and final circle. These concepts have not been thoroughly defined or explored. To divide the EC in two would certainly give rise to formidable institutional and practical difficulties. The idea is not welcome to some aspirants for membership, who feel that they would be being offered second-class citizenship. It is disliked, too, by pro-Europeans in Britain, who fear that a British government might actually prefer the outer circle or that, by its attitude, Britain would be forced into it. But, provided movement from the outer to the inner circle is not ruled out, there are attractions in the concept for countries like Turkey which are manifestly unprepared for the full rigours of the EC rules of the game and are likely to remain so even after a long transitional period. The EC clearly has no intention of allowing the claims of other countries, however pressing, to divert it from the path of closer integration. The more successful that course becomes, the more extensive and demanding the *acquis communautaire*. That will make full membership more difficult for newcomers, however successful their own economic development. Some two-stage process may therefore be inevitable.

Alternative approaches go variously under names such as 'variable geometry' and 'differentiation'. In essence, countries either opt out of or opt in to certain activities (the European Monetary System and the Schengen Group on border controls are prime examples) or else, while committing themselves to a common objective, enjoy some differentiation over the speed or mode by which they arrive at it. Thus for certain parts of the Community agenda there are two tiers or two speeds, and others may follow. The new European Environmental Agency (see Chapter 8) is one such example, where the obligations of membership have yet to be defined and where an added variant is envisaged with the inclusion of non-members, such as the countries of Eastern Europe.

As with a two-tier Europe, it is easier to explain the concept than to see how it would work in practice. It is hard to see how membership could mean anything less than the full obligations of the single market. But what about environmental standards? East Germany is being expected to conform to EC environmental standards with only a relatively short transition for existing plant. Even with a substantial transitional period, these standards will prove a formidable hurdle for the countries of Eastern Europe to jump. But if too much 'differentiation' were allowed, would there not be an unacceptable distortion of competition? One area where differentiation could perhaps be envisaged is 'political cooperation' (see Chapter 4), but the more closely this becomes enmeshed in Community business the more difficult that will become. It might be a convenient device if the EC became more involved in security matters, but that would not be without its difficulties. Although 'differentiation' and 'variable geometry' may continue to be useful tools for the EC in limited cases, they are unlikely to provide the answer to the enlargement dilemma.

For the Community to put up its shutters against further enlargement would be indefensible. For it to prevaricate indefinitely would be unreasonable. It can continue to insist (as it has done in all

27

previous enlargement negotiations) that members must, after a suitable transition, accept the prevailing *acquis communautaire*, but for it to create new conditions would be unfair. On this basis, solutions can no doubt be found to Austria's remaining difficulties over membership if the EEA negotiations fail; certainly there would be no case for delaying the relevant procedures. Other EFTA countries could decide for themselves whether or not to follow suit.

But this will not solve the problems for the non-EFTA candidates because for the moment those requirements are too stiff. The Community should not feel obliged to treat everyone in the same way and certainly not on a first-come-first-served basis. What seems to be the best solution for Eastern Europe (and possibly Turkey) is not a two-tier Europe but some kind of two-phase membership, in which the progress to full membership is much more assured than in the earlier forms of association agreement. For instance, potential members could be included from the outset in the European Parliament and perhaps given observer status in the Council.

There would be strong resistance within the Community to repeating what many saw as the error of the 1963 Treaty of Ankara, which explicitly envisaged eventual full membership for Turkey, and to treating East European countries more favourably than EFTA ones. The trouble is that their needs are different. By and large, EFTA wants the Community's economics but not necessarily its politics. The countries of Eastern Europe want to be politically integrated with the West but do not necessarily embrace – and certainly could not meet the competition from – the free-market system of the EC. Thus the criteria for movement from the preliminary to the final stage of membership would have to be both economic and political, thereby guaranteeing the interests of both the Community and the aspiring countries of Eastern Europe. The Community needs to make an early, generous and realistic offer, even though the time when the conditions for full membership will be fulfilled may be far distant. The Intergovernmental Conference in December 1990 is not too soon to address the institutional issues to which such an offer will give rise.

These are not easy choices for anyone in the Community. If Britain is to find support in espousing enlargement, then it will have to make it abundantly clear that this is not intended as a threat to the deepening of the Community and that Britain will back such moves where they can be justified on merit. In particular, Britain would have to support means to speed up the Community's decision-making processes. It is a fallacy to believe that enlargement would prevent further economic and political integration but leave the achievements of the single market intact. A failure to compensate for the larger numbers by increasing the Community's internal efficiency would be much more likely to mean that substantive British interests, such as the maintenance of free and fair competition and the further liberalization of services, would be stultified than that grandiose calls for European union would be silenced. Far from leading to a weaker Community, it is likely to mean more majority voting and more power for the Commission. This is a choice Britain will have to make.

4

THE EC AND ITS RELATIONS

'He may not, as unvalu'd persons do
'Care for himself, for on his choice depends
'The safety and the health of the whole state'
– HAMLET

As the preceding chapter showed, the EC is the pole of attraction in Europe – by virtue of its position at the centre of a web of interlocking groupings (See Figure 2). The events of the past eighteen months in the Soviet Union and Eastern Europe have started off a process of reappraisal of the role of all these organizations and the policies which they represent. Some must decline in importance; others see themselves with a new role, drawing together those parts of Europe until recently divided by the iron curtain in what Edward Mortimer describes as 'the springtime of the institutions'.[1]

Of all the international bodies affected by the events in Eastern Europe and even more in the Soviet Union, it is NATO which has the most radical rethinking to do. For forty years it has represented the West's side of the cold war. While remaining a defensive alliance, it has now offered the Warsaw Pact a 'joint declaration in which we solemnly state that we are no longer adversaries'.[2] What this will do to the structure of NATO and its links with the EC is discussed later in this chapter. This rethinking will also embrace the Western European Union (WEU), to which most EC members belong. This organization has in recent years served as a convenient forum in which the core European members of NATO, including France (which dropped out of the NATO integrated defence structure in

1966 under de Gaulle), discuss security and to a lesser extent defence matters. The Iraqi conflict may have given the WEU a boost as the forum in which Europe's military response is coordinated.

Figure 2   The EC's organizational friends and neighbours

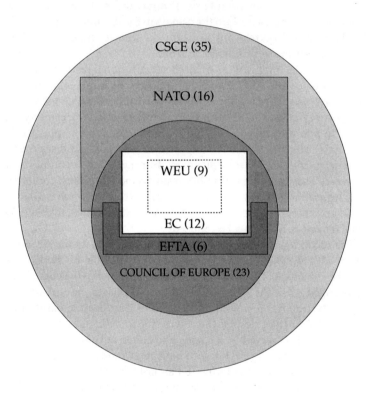

EC12: Belgium, Denmark, France, FRG, Greece, Ireland, Italy, Luxembourg, Netherlands, Portugal, Spain, UK.
EFTA: Austria, Finland, Iceland, Norway, Sweden, Switzerland.
Council of Europe: EC plus EFTA plus Cyprus, Liechtenstein, Malta, San Marino, Turkey.
NATO: EC less Ireland plus Canada, Iceland, Norway, Turkey, USA.
CSCE: Council of Europe plus Bulgaria, Canada, Czechoslovakia, former GDR, the Holy See, Hungary, Monaco, Poland, Romania, USA, USSR, Yugoslavia.
WEU: EC less Denmark, Greece, Ireland.

Finally, the Conference on Security and Cooperation in Europe (CSCE), launched in 1973 as part of the remarkable Helsinki peace process, has been given a wholly new significance by the new spirit of cooperation between East and West. As the body which includes not only the superpowers but virtually all the countries of Europe – 35 in all – it has a strong claim to become 'institutionalized' and strengthened as the umbrella organization able to discuss and handle matters on a pan-European basis. Producing results in such a large body will not be easy, but the tone set by the discussions in the Conference will be relevant not only to security issues but to the EC's relationship with Eastern Europe.

What are the implications of all this institutional restructuring for the EC's place and role? Two general points are important. First, as William Wallace argues, the European institutions which grew up in the postwar period under the shadow of American hegemony are likely to find that they have a more autonomous role to play as the two major alliances decline in importance (and possibly disappear).[3] American military involvement in Europe is a function of a perceived common threat that has been deemed to be best contained on a transatlantic basis. It would be foolish to abandon that alliance while any threat remains. But, as the threat diminishes, the military involvement is bound to be reduced.

The second general point follows from the first. As the strongest and most cohesive force in Europe, the central role of the EC can only be enhanced. This too is a development which is welcomed and encouraged by the United States. Whenever an American administration has reviewed its attitude to European integration, it has concluded that, despite the risk to its commercial interests, the USA will be best served by a strong and cohesive Europe.[4] The Bush administration is only the latest to have re-examined its position and come to the same conclusion. It has not always been a welcome conclusion in Britain, but it is an important reason why Britain has to see its future international influence being exerted less on a national basis and more through the indirect medium of the EC.

These factors were well illustrated by the proposal of the American President at the summit meeting of world leaders in Paris in July 1989 that the EC Commission should be asked to take responsibility for overall coordination of Western assistance to Poland and Hungary. It was also a reminder that the EC will have to play a significant part in the assistance programme for the countries of

Eastern Europe. The decision to set up a European Bank for Reconstruction and Development marks the beginning of what will have to be a major effort by both the private and the public sector. Whether as members of the EC or in some form of special relationship, the countries of Eastern Europe and the Mediterranean are going to represent a substantial call on the financial resources of the EC and its member states. Furthermore, events in both Eastern Europe and the Middle East have added impetus to the debates in the EC about foreign policy collaboration and the case for extending the EC's responsibilities to the defence and security field.

Foreign policy: cooperation or collaboration?

Britain has been one of the major supporters of and contributors to the development of European political cooperation (more properly described as foreign policy cooperation but having entered into the Euro-jargon as EPC). With increasing intensity since the early 1970s, the member states of the EC have discussed together all important questions of foreign policy (other than defence). Kept strictly separate at the outset from EC business, procedures and practices have gradually been brought closer to the EC itself without losing the basic characteristics of EPC: that it proceed only by way of consensus, and that the Presidency rather than the Commission play the leading role. In this way, EPC has, to quote one practitioner, built up 'a formidable system of concertation, which has fundamentally altered the traditional tight-lipped methods of working of foreign policy establishments of earlier generations . . . It helps to explain how, over the last decade or so, it has been the exception rather than the rule for major differences of view over foreign policy issues to become apparent.'[5]

EPC may be said to have come of age when its existence was formally recognized in the Single European Act, again at British instigation. The Act also contained provision for the EPC process to be reviewed in 1992; but an earlier review is desirable in view of the momentous changes which have taken place since the Act was ratified. There seems to be a widespread feeling that the EPC process could and should be pushed further forward. At one extreme the European Parliament sets as a target the achievement of a common foreign policy. This could be understood to mean giving competence to the Community institutions to conduct a single policy for the

Community and replacing national embassies and foreign services by a single body, presumably manned by the Commission, which would be answerable to the Council for the implementation of this as of other common policies. A common foreign policy carried to this degree would probably be unacceptable not only to Britain but also to France. In both countries foreign policy is seen as an essential manifestation of international prestige and national sovereignty. Nevertheless, the British government appears to favour some further strengthening of the existing EPC process and will be joining others in putting its ideas to the IGC, which begins in December 1990. The indications are that nothing very dramatic will emerge beyond improvements to the present procedures.

How far might such improvements go in the interests of efficacy and economy (good yardsticks for a British government)?

There are three stages in the process of foreign policy: the collection and assessment of information and intelligence; the formulation of policy; and finally implementation.

(a) Collection of information

In the present EPC procedure there is a great deal of sharing of information both in overseas posts and in the EPC process itself, but the collection of information is essentially the task of member states. The input is naturally greatest from the larger member states and those that have the closest interest in the issue under consideration. Britain's contribution is widely praised and valued. The Commission's input is negligible, since it has only a very limited number of overseas representatives and their work is naturally focused on aid and trade issues and in countries where those issues of Community competence are important. How far this pooling of information goes is in the end at the discretion of the national governments. There is almost certainly a great deal of duplication, though some of it is useful corroborative evidence. There could well be a case for some division of labour whereby one country takes on responsibility for the whole Community of monitoring one particular area of interest in the country concerned. Carried to its logical conclusion, this would mean in smaller countries that one embassy would undertake the whole of the information-gathering task for the remaining states.

Such a system would work only if there were a clearly laid-down agreement on the dissemination of information to all member states and to the Commission. As things are at the moment, the Commission must increasingly find itself having to represent the Community's position or to take decisions with international implications on the basis of far less intelligence and other forms of relevant information than is available to individual member states through their own diplomatic network. This cannot be of advantage to the Community. The sharing of information needs to be two-way and the exchange of covert intelligence dependent on adequate security precautions.

(b) Formulation of policy

At the level of decision-making or the formulation of policy, the crucial question is whether EPC should remain a process which proceeds by consensus or whether the member states could agree to some form of majority voting. The requirement for consensus has been a considerable handicap, particularly when one recalcitrant country can prevent the EC from speaking with a united voice. The time has come for the introduction of forms of majority decision-making in EPC. A start might be made, for example, with the member states agreeing to abide by a majority decision on how to cast their votes in the UN. It would be possible, at any rate initially, to build in an understanding that, while countries would normally accept a majority decision, some kind of conscience clause would allow for exceptions in particular cases (e.g. for Greece where an issue affecting Cyprus was involved).

There is also a good case for bringing the EPC and the EC processes even closer together. One of the main reasons for speeding up cooperation is that foreign and economic policies are becoming increasingly inseparable. It makes less and less sense to separate the EPC machinery from the economic issues, for which the EC machine has formal responsibility. Although the decision-making processes of EPC and the Community have been brought together at the ministerial level, there is scope for extending this to other levels. In retrospect, the decision of July 1989 to ask the Commission to coordinate policy towards Eastern Europe for the 24 countries involved was a watershed. It has been followed by agreement in July 1990 at the Houston summit that the Commission would work with the International Monetary Fund (IMF) to assess the economic needs of the Soviet Union.

The Commission was not equipped for these tasks but has made strenuous efforts to get up to speed. It has stolen a march on the

EPC. But what is needed is cooperation, not rivalry. There are not many foreign policy issues these days which do not involve consideration of sanctions or trade deals or economic assistance – all areas of EC responsibility. Joint meetings of the relevant working groups should happen much more systematically. At present, the Coreper Ambassadors,* who advise the Council of Ministers on EC issues, and the Political Directors, who advise the same set of ministers on EPC, never meet together. Some way must be found for overcoming the present divide. If the Ambassadors (who are all senior diplomats with wide experience) could delegate more of their present workload to powerful deputies on both the EC and the EPC fronts, then the necessary degree of coordination could be achieved without creating an impossible burden. This, after all, is what foreign ministers achieve. In such an arrangement, the Commission could be treated as an equal partner with the same right to make proposals as any member state. To do so, some modest injection of additional expertise would be required. Giving the EPC Secretariat more staff, both permanent and seconded from national administrations, and making it an integral part of the Council Secretariat, would also help to improve the efficiency of the process. Better arrangements could also be made for Community representation at international gatherings. Where there is mixed competence, there should be one EC delegation jointly led by the Commission and the Presidency.

(c) *Implementation of foreign policy*
If these changes were made as regards information-gathering and decision-making, consequential changes at the level of implementation of foreign policy would follow naturally. If Country A was the source of advice to the whole EC on Country B, its embassy would also be the natural vehicle to represent the interests of all EC countries there. Where there was also a Commission representative, he should be co-located. A possible variant would be to set up EC embassies with staff drawn from two or three member states. Modest attempts by Benelux, France and Germany at shared embassies have not been a great success, but if the Community set in

* Comité des Représentants Permanents. Each member state has its representative, or 'ambassador', to the Community; the committee formed by these representatives tries to get as much agreement as possible on any issue before taking it to the Council of Ministers.

train a systematic programme over a period of years, the practical difficulties would become more manageable. It will no doubt be expedient to proceed gradually, since there are some deep-seated prejudices as well as practical obstacles to be overcome. It might in the event prove more difficult to get countries to share trade promotion than to share diplomatic secrets! But the full benefits in cost-saving and greater effectiveness will not be achieved until the practice becomes widespread.

Prospects
For the foreseeable future, the conduct of foreign policy will continue to involve both the Community as such and the individual member states acting more or less in harmony. This state of affairs calls for the maximum degree of collaboration and the minimum number of demarcation disputes. The present arrangements are far from satisfactory. Britain and the Community as a whole would stand to gain from much closer collaboration. There is no doubt that on most foreign policy issues Britain's interests are similar to, if not identical with, those of its European partners.

The place of the EC in security and defence
In contrast to its somewhat uneasy relationship with its Community partners, Britain has always felt comfortable in the Atlantic atmosphere of NATO and in the role of America's most dependable ally, often acting as an intermediary between the USA and Western Europe. At the same time, however, it has taken a leading role within two bodies concerned with security, the Eurogroup and the Independent European Programme Group (IEPG), as well as in the revitalization of WEU. Collaboration with Germany on a range of security issues is of long standing. Serious attempts to strengthen Anglo-French collaboration have been made by both sides, but have been hampered by misunderstandings and different perceptions of respective security interests. Nevertheless, some progress has been achieved.

Although Britain still maintains extensive links with the United States in intelligence, communications and some specialized military operations, its influence on the US in security and defence, as in other matters, is declining. The American administration has made it abundantly clear that it prefers to see Britain's effort as part of an integrated Europe than in terms of a special UK/US relationship. The balance between the Atlantic and the European framework for British foreign policy has been gradually shifting over the past 30 years, although successive British governments have been slow to recognize or accept the fact. This is the conclusion drawn by one expert:

> Britain should contribute to European efforts to ensure that the links with the USA remain secure, but it now seems likely that Britain will exercise a stronger influence on the USA if she continues to develop and deepen, as an act of policy, her security relations with Europe and if she pursues Atlanticism as an ally and partner within a NATO and EC framework.[6]

The NATO summit meeting in London in July 1990 appeared to endorse the view that the EC had a role to play. In the section of the communiqué dealing with the unification of Germany, the NATO leaders said: 'The move within the European Community towards political union, *including the development of a European identity in the domain of security*, will also contribute to Atlantic solidarity and to the establishment of a just and lasting peace throughout Europe.'[7]

How should that happen? The existing links are of two kinds. The first relates to arms procurement. The continuing existence of an up-to-date defence industry in the EC, capable of competing with the US and other major arms suppliers, can be seen as an important part of the Community's industrial strategy. It would help to speed up the slow process of collaboration between EC countries if the present exemption of defence projects from the EC's procurement directive were withdrawn. This should be considered, even though it would cause another trade row with the US.

The second link is with EPC, where it is argued that movement towards a common foreign policy requires movement towards a common security policy. The Gulf crisis has added urgency to the issue. What conclusions should be drawn from the obvious disarray in the way individual EC countries reacted initially to the Iraqi invasion of Kuwait? Does the lack-lustre response among EC countries prove the impracticability of proper defence collaboration among them and suggest that WEU is the better forum in which to coordinate action outside the NATO area? Or should it lead, as the Italians have proposed, to the creation of new machinery within the

EC capable of producing a speedy security response? Sir Leon Brittan has proposed the creation of a European Security Community which would subsume WEU and the IEPG and become as close a part of the EC constellation as the differing memberships would allow.[8]

At this stage, the overriding need, accepted by everyone in Europe, is to retain US involvement with effective forces on the ground in Europe. This suggests that it would be wise to consider first the future of NATO and what role the CSCE might play before deciding on the creation of new permanent structures from which the US might feel distanced. Nevertheless, the Gulf crisis has accelerated the process of evaluation and, as the security problems of Europe come to be reassessed, the case for a specifically European body will be established and the form it should take will become clearer. What is certain is that the interplay between foreign policy, economic policy and security is becoming greater all the time. It is therefore inevitable that EPC, and to a lesser extent the Community institutions, already find themselves touching on security questions. To ensure that this happens in an informed way, and that there is no duplication of effort as NATO in turn becomes increasingly concerned with non-Soviet threats, the EC should establish better links with NATO – both through EPC channels and by strengthening communication between the Commission and the NATO Secretariat. As the EC acquires more familiarity and expertise, it would need to consider whether it would be preferable to preserve WEU and strengthen its links with the Community or to seek to absorb the work of WEU into the EPC process. It does not seem likely that the problem of the 'neutrals' would present a major difficulty in the latter solution. Much more significant would be the way in which the defence issues surrounding Germany – the reason WEU was set up in the first place – are to be dealt with in the new security structure.

Bilateral relations

Throughout its life, the EC has been dominated by the Franco-German alliance. The Franco-German Treaty of 1963 has led over the years to a real thickening of contacts between the two administrations and an increasing ability to present a combined front in Brussels. This has been a source of great strength to them and of frequent annoyance to the other member states. Britain has never succeeded in substituting a triangular relationship of anything like the same strength, partly because it arrived late in the Community, but chiefly because it gave priority to the Anglo-American relationship. The result has been a source of weakness within the EC, and as a stance for Britain it has now become outmoded. Today, across virtually the whole spectrum of foreign and security policy issues, London's relations with Bonn and Paris have become every bit as important as those with Washington. The Gulf crisis may constitute one of the exceptions, but it does not change the rule. It is a fact which is not yet been fully understood in Britain.

As with so much else under discussion here, events in Eastern Europe, and especially the unification of Germany, have put strains on the Franco-German alliance, although it is still a potent force in the EC. Valéry Giscard d'Estaing, the former French president, has suggested that Germany's priorities are now relations with the USA and with the Soviet Union, and that 'Franco-German intimacy is no longer at the centre of the process of European union'.[9] This piece of hyperbole reflected concern about the state of the relationship and underlying French worries from way back about German unification. On the German side there may be a desire to exploit the new situation in order to extract a less idiosyncratic attitude from France on how to handle Europe's security.

There should be a new opportunity for Britain to improve its bilateral relations with France so as to promote more effectively the important interests which the two countries share. Their security interests are basically the same. Both are nuclear powers, with approximately equal capabilities in nuclear and conventional weapons. Neither wishes prematurely to drop its guard until the changes in Soviet policy are seen to be irreversible. Both have overseas involvements and a colonial past. Both have an interest in containing the new Germany. Current differences are as much about history and posturing as they are about substance. It must be right to foster not only closer nuclear and other defence collaboration but much more widespread political cooperation as well. It is high time for a major reappraisal of Anglo-French relations by a high-level commission enjoying the confidence of both governments.[10]

The Anglo-German relationship will continue to be crucial. Although relations are basically sound, the two countries are not close at the political level. Personality clashes and relatively minor differences on industrial management appear to have prevented greater exploitation within the EC of the ideological similarities between Thatcherism and German economic liberalism. Nor has the Atlanticism of the two governments done much to foster a closer working relationship. So there is an important relationship here to be worked at and some political fences to be mended. In public Germany may have shrugged off official expressions of distaste for German unification, but good relations must have been impaired. Such remarks in any case belie the realities of modern Anglo-German relations, which are in fact based upon a large number of shared interests. There is a high level of trust now felt in Britain towards Germany, a country which occupies too significant a place within Europe for any British government to neglect.

Important as these two relationships are, the Community requires the constant nurturing of contacts with all Community partners. In Brussels, Britain well understands the tactical game of alliances and plays it well. But the foundations for such diplomacy are laid at the strategic level and in the personal links between ministers and officials in capitals. Attention paid to one of the smaller member states often produces quite disproportionate dividends when it comes to bargaining around the Council table. Britain has a particular need to cultivate closer links with the southern member states, especially Italy and Spain, which constitute an important element in the EC, even if some of their interests may be different from its own. However, it will be difficult to form strategic alliances with these countries – as it will be with France and Germany – unless Britain can show convincingly that, like them, it is serious about European integration.[11]

5

1992 AND ALL THAT

'I think he bought his doublet in Italy,
'his roundhose in France, his bonnet in
'Germany, and his behaviour everywhere'
— THE MERCHANT OF VENICE

British enthusiasm for the single market is not difficult to understand. For the Conservative government under Mrs Thatcher, it seemed largely in accord with its own free-market philosophy. 'If the problems of growth, outdated industrial structures and unemployment which affect us all are to be tackled effectively, we must create the genuine common market in goods and services which is envisaged in the Treaty of Rome and will be crucial to our ability to meet the US and Japanese technological challenge.'[1] What was good for Britain must be good for Europe. Indeed, because Britain had led the way, some EC thinking on liberalization has been able to draw on British experience; in the financial services sector, in particular, much of the EC liberalization programme is modelled on British legislation and practice.

This positive attitude has been strongly endorsed by the bulk of British industry and commerce. Having themselves been perforce exposed to the bracing winds of competition, British companies wanted the same medicine applied to their Community partners. Moreover, there were genuine market opportunities to be exploited, particularly by the financial services sector, which by and large felt it had a competitive advantage and where protective practices elsewhere in the EC were particularly rife. For the larger British companies, the prospect of an EC-wide domestic market provided the base they needed to operate effectively on a world-wide scale. Finally, the beginnings of the 1992 programme coincided with a period when the British economy was performing well in comparison with the rest of the EC and business confidence was high. The more recent reversal in the relative performance of the British and other EC economies has undoubtedly affected business confidence, but the sense that there is no other option but to press on with the EC liberalization remains. The government can therefore count on the continued support of the business sector.

The Conservative government's support for the single market has, however, its limits. When Lord Cockfield argued that the harmonization of VAT rates was essential to the free movement of goods, he touched on the raw nerve of sovereignty. It would be acceptable for the market to force governments to adjust their VAT rates so as to avoid trade distortions, but not for the rates to be set or even constrained by EC rules for harmonization. In this respect, the Labour Party took the same attitude as the government. In general, the Labour Party has been unenthusiastic about the 1992 programme, believing it to be too free-market in concept and to take insufficient account of the need for the EC to have a more active Europe-wide industrial policy.[2] Since several other countries took the same view as Britain on the question of tax harmonization, the Commission has temporarily backed off, but it seems certain that the issues will re-emerge in some form or other before very long.

Because the political significance of the 1992 programme is so great, a tremendous effort will no doubt be made (with Britain holding the Presidency in the second half of 1992 and pulling out all the stops) to ensure that the Community reaches some decisions on all the outstanding Commission proposals by the due date. Doubtless this pressure will result in some flimsy compromises and muddles, as indeed has been the case with some of the more difficult questions on which decisions have already been reached.

Revisiting the single market
Perhaps one should regard the internal market programme as being rather like painting the Forth Bridge: initial moves at liberalization will be seen not to have gone far enough or to require modification in one way or another. Take, for instance, the field of transpor-

tation. Measures are in process of being adopted which will lead to the liberalization of road and air transport; but it seems unlikely that all national restrictions will have disappeared by the end of 1992. The same looks like being true of some classes of insurance. Another round of liberalization will be needed and should be started as soon as the present programme has been completed.

Another area in which Britain has important interests and on which the last word has certainly not been said is mergers policy.[3] It is generally acknowledged that the Merger Control Regulation – eventually adopted by the Council in December 1989 – though a substantial advance towards clarifying the respective roles of the Community and national regulatory authorities, is likely to require revision in the light of experience. There are ambiguities in the text. One of the aims of the regulation – to avoid firms being exposed to the double jeopardy of scrutiny by both national and Community authorities – has not been achieved. And it has already been agreed that the criteria for deciding whether a merger should be considered nationally or by the EC will be revised so as to put more responsibility on the Community authorities.

Britain fought hard and successfully, along with Germany, to ensure that the EC regulation made competition the dominant consideration in judging whether mergers should be allowed. This corresponds with current British policy; but it would not necessarily suit some future government wishing to give more weight to other criteria, such as the need for Europe-wide firms better able to meet Japanese and American competition. A related issue of great concern in Britain is the so-called 'level playing-field'. Although merger activity takes place throughout the EC, and the British are as active acquirers as anybody, British companies are much more exposed to takeover than their Continental counterparts because of Britain's legal and financial set-up.[4] This is felt by many to be unfair competition, and it is likely that any revision of the merger regulation will be linked by Britain to provisions ensuring a more level playing-field between British-registered companies and foreign ones.

Implementation

It is one thing for the Commission to propose and the Council to decide; it is another thing for those decisions to be carried out. In the first place, since many of the decisions take the form of directives, rather than directly applicable regulations, each member state has to enact an implementing measure according to its own legislative procedures. Britain has an excellent record of speedy implementation and has campaigned for improvement among its partners. There is concern that the economic benefits of liberalization will be neither maximized nor evenly shared if the provisions are not implemented by all member states. Italy, for example, has a parliamentary system which has been unable to cope with the volume of Community legislation that the 1992 programme has generated. It is now making changes in those procedures in an attempt to speed up the process of implementation. The problem of implementation is likely to be addressed at the Intergovernmental Conference on institutional issues (see Chapter 9). More use could be made of directly applicable regulations; or, alternatively, provision might be made that, if directives are not implemented within a defined period, they would be made directly applicable in the member states concerned, thus avoiding the need for additional national legislation.

The IGC will also address a second, and probably more serious, cause for concern over compliance with decisions already taken. Either through inefficiency or because the member state has no enthusiasm for the decision, it will be implemented only partially or ineffectively, or not at all. When this happens, the other member states are put at a disadvantage. As regards compliance, Britain cannot stand in a completely white sheet (notably on the environmental front, where its relatively few failures, such as water quality and the safety of beaches, inevitably attract media attention) but nevertheless has a better record than most. At the moment, it is the Commission's task to monitor the implementation of Community legislation. It can complain to the offending member state, but if it cannot get satisfaction its only recourse is to the European Court. This is a lengthy process, and, even if it secures a Court judgment, there is often a long period of prevarication before the matter is put right. This is a cause of growing concern, especially in Britain. There is a good case for amending the Treaties to allow the imposition of financial or other penalties on offending member states. To be effective, there would have to be some quick procedure for the Commission to get authorization from the European Court to punish the offender – perhaps by withholding monies due from the Community budget.

In short, it would be wholly wrong to believe that the 1992 programme will somehow complete the EC's internal agenda. The achievement of a single market is itself an ongoing process. Later chapters in this study will deal with major additional items on the Community's agenda; the remainder of this chapter picks up other subjects, both internal and external, with which the Community will be concerned during the next few years.

The Community budget
The EC spends about 45 billion ecus, just over 1% of the Community's GDP. In 1988, the European Council agreed that spending could rise to 1.2% of GDP by 1992, and the Council and the European Parliament subsequently endorsed a financial perspective showing the budget rising to 54 billion ecus in 1992 (at constant prices). The proportion spent on agriculture is expected to decline marginally, and that for the regional, social and other structural funds to double (see Figure 3). Britain contributes 16% of the Community's income, after receiving a rebate under the deal struck in 1984 (see Chapter 2).

With the buoyancy of the European economy, the Community may have sufficient funds within the ceiling to meet its obligations up to 1992, even taking into account the new obligations to help Eastern Europe.[5] But sooner or later the demand to increase the Community budget will come. Britain will find itself in difficulty. Some of the demands which will come from the Commission, the European Parliament and other member states, the current British government would predictably resist: regional assistance to help the weaker regions cope with economic and monetary union; more Community expenditure on educational and research programmes; public investment in transport infrastructure – all strong runners. But given its general political posture towards Eastern Europe (and eventually towards the Soviet Union), Britain will find it more difficult to resist claims for increased aid to help redevelopment in these areas. Far from producing windfall savings (as it did in 1989), the world market is likely to cause agricultural expenditure to start shooting up again.

A new government, particularly a Labour government, might look more favourably on an expanded EC budget; but Britain's general reluctance to see higher expenditure is likely to persist. So is

Figure 3   EC budget 1989

(a) Where it goes:

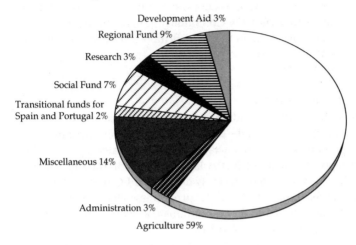

Development Aid 3%
Regional Fund 9%
Research 3%
Social Fund 7%
Transitional funds for Spain and Portugal 2%
Miscellaneous 14%
Administration 3%
Agriculture 59%

(b) Who pays:

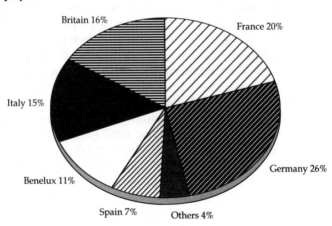

Britain 16%
France 20%
Italy 15%
Germany 26%
Benelux 11%
Spain 7%
Others 4%

Source: HM Treasury (Cm 1059).

the belief that Community expenditure always means additional national expenditure, whereas, with the help of the Treasury, it often merely substitutes for national expenditure and thus represents no net addition to the taxpayer's burden. The size of the Community budget, what it should be spent on and its redistributive effects on each member state (an issue discussed in Chapter 7) are all subjects which are likely to occupy the Community at regular intervals in the future, as they have done in the past. Britain will be in the thick of the argument, but unlikely to be isolated.

Trade policy in the 1990s

Britain, with its historic trading links, its continued heavy involvement in third-country trade and its strong interest in improved access, particularly for financial services, has always been the keenest supporter, with the Netherlands, of a liberal trading posture for the EC. Two issues have recently dominated EC trade policy: the external implications of the 1992 programme and the Uruguay Round of international trade negotiations under the General Agreement on Tariffs and Trade (GATT).

The Community's single market initiative was launched without much thought for the effects on third countries. Nor did the rest of the world show much interest until the Commission injudiciously introduced a 'reciprocity' clause into its proposals for liberalizing banking services within the EC – a move which led the Americans in particular to fear that they would be excluded from the EC market because their domestic arrangements did not seem to the EC to provide adequate access for Community banks.[6] This storm in a teacup was eventually ended by a text so bland that it offended nobody. Nevertheless, it provoked exaggerated charges that the 1992 programme was going to turn the EC into Fortress Europe, charges which, though much abated, still fly around. In fact third countries should benefit both directly from the removal of internal barriers (a single application for patent rights throughout the EC, for example) and indirectly from the growth of the single market induced by their removal. The only legitimate fear is that the increased competition within the EC will lead to greater pressures for external protection.

Some evidence that this is happening can be seen in the extensive – and many would say excessive – use by the Community of anti-dumping provisions against imports, chiefly from the newly industrialized countries. By and large, however, the Commission's record in resisting protectionist pressures is a creditable one and owes something to the unfaltering support it has had from the British. How the Commission responds to the pressure from European car manufacturers for strict controls on Japanese car imports post-1992 will be a crucial test.

Some of the external issues which have arisen as a result of the 1992 programme – as, for example, the harmonization of standards – are likely to be tackled in the context of the Uruguay Round. Indeed its coincidence with this phase of the 1992 programme has been a godsend in taking some of the heat out of potentially contentious issues, including the rules governing resort to anti-dumping duties. The Uruguay Round of negotiations, much the most complex attempted by the GATT, is due to be completed in December 1990. Britain has been active in seeking a successful outcome and has been especially constructive in finding ways to introduce liberalization into the trade in services and in combining the efforts of the private sector and the official negotiators.

As a major trading bloc, the EC has much to gain from a successful outcome. The enhancement of trade opportunities and the prospect of better safeguards (e.g. for intellectual property) will benefit all Community countries, not least Britain. Conversely, a failure in the Uruguay Round would greatly increase the risk not only of widespread protectionism but of the US abandoning the whole multilateral trading system in favour of a bilateral approach. There is much at stake for all the major players, including the EC. Internal differences among the member states have so far not prevented the Community from being a strong supporter of the open trading system and the GATT. But this has been possible only because of strong British backing. On most of the issues under negotiation in the Uruguay Round, the Community has occupied a reasonably central position. There is, however, one area – widely felt to be critical to the success of the entire round – where it has frequently been challenged under the GATT rules and where it is in the firing-line. This is agriculture.

Pressure on the CAP
The Common Agricultural Policy has long been regarded in Britain

as one of the worst features of the EC. Accepted with great reluctance (except by the farmers) when Britain joined, it has been the aim of successive British governments to bring about reform of its worst features – namely, the creation of expensive and unwanted surpluses and the imposition of heavy costs on both consumers and taxpayers. With the rapid escalation in costs in the early 1980s leading to the absorption of up to three-quarters of the entire Community budget, some success was achieved and limits were put both on the volume of production and on the amount of budgetary expenditure. Sustained British pressure contributed largely to this result.

The Community's wish to reform the CAP coincided with equal concern in other parts of the world at the rising level of agricultural subsidization and the distortions that this was creating for world trade. Hence it was easy to get all the participants to agree at the start of the Uruguay Round that a serious attempt should be made to cut agricultural subsidies and try to bring agriculture more effectively within the disciplines of the GATT.

This has not prevented major disagreements emerging as to what should or should not be done. The US, with a powerful agricultural sector, has pressed for the elimination of all forms of support for agricultural production and has been especially critical of the EC's system of export subsidies. The EC, while ready to make reductions in agricultural subsidies on a multilateral basis, is unwilling to dismantle the CAP or to expose its diverse and often small-scale and inefficient farming to the world market. Britain, on the liberal wing of the EC spectrum (but not wholly unmindful of its farming constituency), has sought to push the Community into taking up a respectable negotiating position. While a failure to agree cannot be ruled out, the most likely outcome is a package that will do something to tighten the disciplines on agricultural trade and produce a programme of phased reductions in those forms of agricultural support which distort trade. This will certainly not remove all sources of possible conflict between the EC and the US, but it may be the start of a GATT process which will exert some external pressure to moderate the worst excesses of the CAP.

Such a process will find reinforcement from within the EC. Environmental concerns (discussed more fully in Chapter 8) will put pressure on the more intensive farming methods. The preservation and development of the countryside for ecological and recreational purposes will provide alternative sources of income for farmers. With its Environmentally Sensitive Areas scheme, Britain has led the thinking within the EC on ways to encourage environmentally friendly types of farming. Attitudes in Germany – long the staunchest defender of the worst features of the CAP – may change as the potentially highly productive large farms of East Germany become properly organized, bringing Germany more in line with the efficient agriculture of France and the UK. And when agriculture starts once again to make disproportionate claims on the Community budget as a result of over-production or low world prices, then the pressure for more CAP reform will be renewed.

Each of these developments is thus likely to shift the CAP in the direction of more exposure to market forces (including the abolition of the infamous system of 'monetary compensatory amounts', which has been a major cause of distortion)[7] and towards the use of more clearly differentiated policy instruments to meet the social, economic and environmental needs of rural areas. These developments accord wholly with British interests. Britain should press for a price policy which links EC prices much more closely to what is happening on world markets and for a shift in policy away from market support to a properly differentiated set of policies for the rural areas. It should try to resist the political pressure from the farming lobbies to retain special support for small farmers or peripheral areas in ways which distort the market.

Freedom at the frontiers?

Britain has argued that the statement in the Single European Act that 'the internal market shall comprise an area without internal frontiers' does not require the abolition of all frontier controls.[8] With what is largely a sea frontier, it is understandable that Britain should rate more highly than Continental countries the advantages of using frontier checks as one of the weapons in the fight against terrorism, illegal immigration and drugs. But it should be acknowledged that, once again, the concern over national sovereignty has added heat to what is in any case a complex issue.

It is in the area of border controls, therefore, that the EC seems most likely to find itself with a two-speed Community. The members of the so-called Schengen group,* after intense negotiation, have agreed to abolish many of the border controls operating between their five countries, with the beginning of 1992 as the target-date for implementation. In order to achieve this, they are in the process of devising new methods of police cooperation and cross-border operations, and ways to deal with extradition, penalties for drugs, visa policy and, most recently, the problems created by the new unified German border with Eastern Europe. Other EC countries, notably Italy and Spain, have expressed a wish to join the Schengen group; but, even if one or two members have been added by the time the border controls are lifted, there is certainly no chance that it will embrace the whole Community. While in general opposed to arrangements involving only some member states, the Commission has condoned the Schengen process on the understanding that the group is merely anticipating what the Commission wishes to see achieved on a Community-wide basis.

In the meantime, Britain has not been idle in developing ways to simplify its own border checks, as travellers through Heathrow or the Channel ports will have noticed. Indeed it is not always appreciated that some of the British systems are now less obtrusive than those employed by, say, the French or the Belgians, and that the differences are often more of rhetoric than of substance. At the practitioner level, the 'honesty and realism' of British officials commands respect,[9] but at the political level this sometimes comes across as opposition to the whole exercise.

Much of what is being developed by the Schengen group in terms of closer cross-border cooperation is being carefully followed by the British police and other enforcement agencies. There is need for more objective study of the real importance of the border check in the fight against crime and the extent to which rivalry between different services may itself be an obstacle to change. In the view of one British expert, 'Our inherited border controls provide a false sense of security and run the risk of becoming obstacles to the fight against transnational crime, traffic in arms and drugs and illegal immigration.'[10] Moreover, it seems certain that the sheer growth in the volume of traffic in goods and people, as well as lobbying from travellers and traders if they find conditions easier elsewhere, will

* Named after the Luxembourg border village where, in June 1985, the talks on closer cross-border cooperation began. The group consists of France, West Germany and the Benelux countries.

put pressure on Britain for further relaxation. Animal and plant health controls will remain a particularly difficult area, since here there may be a convincing case for exploiting the existence of the Channel – e.g. against rabies – even after the Tunnel has opened. A balance has to be struck between the interests and convenience of traders and travellers, the effectiveness of legitimate controls, and 'the quest for the frontier-free ideal' leading to 'more expensive, bureaucratic and generally inconvenient ways' of operating than existed previously.[11]

In finding the right balance for Britain, a more positive political direction from the government would help to achieve quicker and better results. Despite constant public pronouncements by both the Commission and the government about the importance of creating a 'Citizens' Europe', the EC has lamentably failed to fire the imagination of most ordinary people; and nowhere more so than in Britain. The many cultural efforts being made on a cross-national or European level will help. So will the increased freedom of movement, whether for work or for pleasure. The highly successful COMMETT and ERASMUS schemes to encourage student exchanges within the EC will undoubtedly bear fruit in the long term.[12] Indeed the importance of education in general to successful European integration can hardly be overemphasized.[13] For industry as well as for the wider public, a greater facility with European languages must rank high among educational priorities. So should ensuring that both management and workforce are equipped to face the competition from a highly trained Japan or America. That is certainly the view of European industrialists;[14] and if more involvement on the part of the EC in technical and other forms of training can help to improve Britain's record, then it should be encouraged. The application of the subsidiarity principle will always mean that much of education remains a national or a local responsibility, but Britain could well take a lead in encouraging more active cooperation at Community level.

This chapter has dealt with a number of questions which will occupy the EC over the next few years – all of them of major concern to Britain. The list is not exhaustive. It is possible to think of many other issues which could arise. For instance, how far will the Community go into newer areas such as health, social security or direct taxation? What will be the research priorities for the coming decade? How are national aids to be controlled? What about overseas aid policy and the present split between national and Community aid programmes? How should the Community's relations with the African, Caribbean and Pacific (ACP) countries develop?[15] Simply to list such questions is to demonstrate how wide and varied are the matters with which the Community has to deal. Whether driven by the Commission, by the member states or by events, they will have to be fitted into the Community's crowded agenda, along with the top-priority ones which form the subject-matter for separate chapters of this study.

6
WHO'S AFRAID OF THE EMU?

> 'O my ducats. O my daughter'
> — THE MERCHANT OF VENICE

Much the most important and potentially divisive item currently on the Community's agenda is the attempt to design and build an economic and monetary union (EMU). Earlier attempts to set up an EMU found either the political climate not ripe or economic circumstances unpropitious. The current move seems to have a greater chance of success, and an Intergovernmental Conference has been called for December 1990 to negotiate the necessary Treaty amendments. The impetus derives from three main factors:

- a desire to carry the Community forward in the rapidly changing conditions that have followed the revolutions in Eastern Europe, and, in particular, to lock a united and economically powerful Germany into the European system;
- the acknowledged success of the European Monetary System (EMS) in reducing exchange-rate fluctuations and achieving greater convergence of inflation rates; and
- the belief that the full economic benefits of the single market will not be realized without certainty over exchange rates.

The Community invited a Committee of Central Bank Governors, presided over by Jacques Delors, to advise on the means of achieving EMU. Their report, known as the Delors Report,[1] envisaged a three-stage approach:

- *Stage I* (which has now been agreed) would strengthen the existing European Monetary System (EMS) by bringing all member states (including Britain) into the exchange-rate mechanism (ERM); it would also strengthen economic and fiscal cooperation (although there are no binding rules);
- *Stage II* would begin with the creation of a new European System of Central Banks (or 'Eurofed', for short) and would be a 'training process', using the new institutions but still allowing exchange-rate adjustments (albeit only in exceptional circumstances);
- *Stage III* would complete the process: exchange rates would be irrevocably fixed or (as is now favoured) there would be a single currency; and domestic and external monetary policy would become the responsibility of the Eurofed.

While these ideas have since been modified and there are still major differences over the mechanics, the approach is broadly accepted by all member states with the exception of Britain.

British views
Britain has a long history of distaste for the management of economic and monetary policy becoming a Community responsibility. In the debates leading up to entry, parliament was regularly assured that economic and financial policies would remain strictly under national control. This did not stop Prime Minister Edward Heath from subscribing to the statement in the Heads of Government communiqué of 19–20 October 1972 that 'the Member States are determined to strengthen the Community by establishing an economic and monetary union, the guarantee of stability and growth, the foundation of their solidarity and the indispensable basis for social progress'.[2] Similar verbal genuflections to 'economic and monetary union' have been made from time to time ever since.

The reality has been different. In 1975, in the White Paper reporting on the outcome of the renegotiation process, the Callaghan government was able to note, with relief, that 'the programme for movement towards full EMU by 1980 . . . was over-ambitious and unattainable'.[3] When in 1977 Roy Jenkins as President of the European Commission, Giscard d'Estaing and

Helmut Schmidt came up with the idea of the European Monetary System, the government was equally unenthusiastic. The Treasury never had any serious intentions of allowing sterling to form part of the core exchange-rate mechanism. Neither the change of government in 1979 nor the somewhat contradictory arguments advanced to explain and defend the position altered the determination to keep sterling out of the ERM.[4] Attitudes began to change only when disenchantment with Britain's own monetary policies set in, and when the ERM was seen to be having considerable success both in stabilizing exchange rates (there has been no real EMS realignment since January 1987) and in holding down inflation in such countries as France and Ireland. The strength of both these arguments bore fruit in the belated decision to take sterling into the ERM with effect from 8 October 1990. While universally welcomed in Britain and the rest of the EC, the decision carried with it no commitment by the government as regards the more far-reaching plans for EMU. Indeed, there is a suspicion that the virtues of the EMS came to be acknowledged only when the spectre of EMU emerged.

Britain's negative reaction to the findings of the Delors Committee therefore came as no surprise. The report undoubtedly contained flaws and, as discussed later in this chapter, there are genuine economic and political problems associated with locking sterling into EMU. Nevertheless, it is clear that, whatever the merits of the arguments, the underlying reason for the government's response had most to do with sovereignty and the belief that the management of the economy, and especially the management of the exchange rate, is too close to the heart of domestic politics to be shared with the rest of the Community. In spite of the fact that, in reality, parliament has very little say in the conduct of monetary policy, this view was widely endorsed on both sides of the House of Commons in a debate on EMU on 2 November 1989. The same concern is reflected in the attitude towards foreign ownership of banks, a concern which has noticeably subsided in recent years with regard to other forms of foreign investment in Britain and the takeover of British companies.

It is also interesting to contrast the British attitude on EMU with what has happened historically over commercial or trade policy. In the mercantilist world of the nineteenth century, external commercial policy was close to the centre of British politics. The Corn Laws could make or break governments. Even this century, Britain willingly accepted the discipline of the gold standard while clinging firmly to the freedom to negotiate, for example, on Imperial Preferences.* Yet after the Second World War, Britain supported the drive for trade liberalization through the GATT and similarly, when it joined the EC, accepted without demur the transfer of responsibility for commercial trade policy to the Commission. In other words, at some point along the road it had no longer become essential for Britain to retain sovereignty over trade policy. Had this not been the case, Britain could never have subscribed to a common market. No one now questions that Britain's trade interests are dealt with on a Community basis or argues that this is politically unacceptable (even when the Community line is not much liked). But over monetary matters the present British parliament takes a different view.

The British government, having failed to block the Delors Report at the 1989 Madrid summit, came forward later that year with a totally different approach, based on a system of competing currencies.[5] This was seen as a delaying tactic and received very little support elsewhere in the EC or indeed among the business community in the UK. Subsequently, the government put forward different proposals for Stage II, whereby a new 'hard' ecu would be managed by a European Monetary Fund in such a way that it would be the strongest, and thus progressively the preferred, currency within the Community.[6] The advantages seen for the 'hard' ecu are:

(a) while creating from the outset a genuine new currency (which the present ecu is not), it allows the market to determine how rapidly this should replace existing national currencies, and hence the point at which it could become the single EC currency;
(b) it represents a genuine half-way house by retaining the separate national central banks but allowing a central body to be set up at an early stage and acquire experience in managing a European currency;
(c) it would create incentives for stiffer monetary policies and lower inflation, thus encouraging the conditions for successful union;
(d) there could be no two-speed EC.

The presentation of these ideas, though marred by an apparent difference of view between the Prime Minister and the Chancellor of

---

* The system of Imperial, or Commonwealth, preferences, covered by various pieces of legislation between 1919 and 1958, allowed certain imports into the UK from Commonwealth countries at preferential rates of customs duties.

the Exchequer as to whether the 'hard' ecu could or ever would become the Community's single currency, brought Britain back into the game. But they still left a gap between Britain and the other EC countries. Admittedly, as the discussion has moved into technicalities and with the uncertainties created by the Gulf crisis, the early political enthusiasm for speedy progress towards the final goal of a single currency has ebbed. Divided counsels have emerged, in particular in Germany (see Chapter 10). Nevertheless, the prevailing mood among EC members is that EMU represents the next logical and desirable step in the integration process; that a *de jure* European monetary system, even if dominated by Germany, is preferable to a *de facto* Deutschmark zone; and that the planned IGC should make treaty provision for it. In Britain, the financial services sector, and much of the business community generally agree that EMU is desirable and are fearful of the consequences if Britain is left behind.

Monetary union

What, then, is the value of EMU? The Commission argues that the elimination of exchange-rate uncertainties will improve the business climate, that a system based on the reputation of Germany for monetary stability will help to control inflation, that greater coordination will make for sounder budgetary policies (but will enable governments to borrow more cheaply), and that the ecu will become a major international currency which will benefit both business and the EC in international coordination. It also believes that there are no a priori grounds for assuming that the overall pattern of gains and losses will not be evenly spread; for this reason, it has declined to propose any further increase in the Community's regional and structural funds (as provided in the case of the 1992 programme) for the benefit of the weaker economies. Overall, the Commission is confident that EMU is a positive-sum game – although it has declined to offer any quantified assessment of the likely benefits.

From the point of view of the traveller and the trader, the convenience of a single currency is manifest. By appropriate hedging, businesses can do a certain amount to reduce the effects of exchange-rate fluctuation, but there is a widespread belief among industrialists in Britain, as in other EC countries, that the benefits of a single market will be greatly enhanced if transactions, whether for the individual holiday-maker or the multinational corporation, can take place on the basis of a single currency.[7]

However, these visible benefits are less significant than the macroeconomic impact. Monetary union means that individual member states no longer have under their control one of the classic instruments of economic policy: the exchange rate. This has traditionally been the way for countries to correct trade imbalances and international competitivity. Unless, therefore, the economic performance of the member states is reasonably uniform, strains and stresses are likely to appear. This could present a particular problem for Britain. Work done by the National Institute for Economic and Social Research (NIESR) suggests that Britain (and to a lesser extent Italy) would have difficulty with fixed exchange rates for some years to come because of the likely continued divergence in its economic performance as compared with most of the rest of the EC.[8] If correct, this would provide at least economic grounds for a two-speed EMU, with the most convergent currencies taking the first step and the remaining member states (including Britain) joining later.

There are, however, two considerations to be set against this view. In the first place, many economists would now question – for a number of reasons, including the growing importance of capital flows – the efficiency of exchange-rate changes in achieving lasting adjustments. The ability to devalue will help to raise employment and output in a poorly performing country only if it produces real changes (e.g. to wages) – and experience suggests that this rarely happens. The conclusion to be drawn is that 'if exchange rates are becoming less powerful as a policy instrument and, at the same time, more volatile, then a smaller country can reduce exchange-rate uncertainty for its businesses and consumers while losing little scope in economic management by linking its currency to that of a large trading bloc'.[9]

This leads on to the second, less tangible consideration. Would an announced decision by Britain that it intended fully to participate in the EMU process from the outset in itself make the process easier? Could forcing the pace of monetary union work in the way that it has appeared to work for the completion of the internal market? Again, the modelling done by the NIESR suggests that it might produce more rapid convergence on inflation for Britain, but that it would have little effect on growth or employment.[10] The economic case for Britain joining the EC in the early 1970s was made on the basis that the unquantifiable 'dynamic' effects of entry were sufficiently foreseeable to more than offset the known and quantifiable static costs.[11] Perhaps a similar phenomenon will work in the case of monetary union. This must, however, be largely speculation. Part of the answer lies in the other side of the EMU medal.

Economic union

It seems likely that the 'E' in EMU will not feature greatly in the IGC discussions. This is partly because no institutional changes are thought to be necessary, and partly because there has been a general disposition in recent years to allow economic union to play second fiddle to monetary union. The Delors Report envisages little more than a tightening-up of the existing machinery for the coordination of macroeconomic policies and discipline in budgetary policy. Member states will be expected to take into account the implications of their national economic policies for the rest of the Community, but not to subject these policies to decision at Community level.

To monetary economists, this contrast between the full integration of monetary policies and the mere coordination of economic policies will not be the occasion for much remark. Control over the money supply, interest-rate policy and overall fiscal probity will appear to cover the essentials of economic management. Neo-Keynesian economists, on the other hand, may question whether such an approach would be sufficient to support the management of the Community economy, with fixed or almost fixed exchange rates, in a way which would maximize sustainable growth, reduce unemployment and secure balanced development throughout the Community. They would point to the fact that there are already major imbalances within the Community, not only in growth performance but in balance-of-payments terms. It is argued, for example, that the scale of the West German surplus, coupled with the paucity of long-term capital outflows, imposes a fundamental asymmetry on national economic policies (although wrestling with the needs of East Germany will greatly alter that picture).[12] Because deficit countries are forced to deflate whereas there is no incentive (or obligation) for the surplus country to expand, the result may be that long-term growth performance in the Community is lower than it could be. This can be corrected only if interregional transfers to sustain high levels of activity are organized throughout the Community.

Against these concerns, economists of the right argue that market forces will bring about the necessary equilibria; that, provided labour costs are not artificially pushed up by unwanted public intervention, capital will flow to the less prosperous parts of the Community (as it has been doing, notably to Spain); that improvements in infrastructure and the long-term decline in the real cost of transport will improve the position of peripheral areas; that resource transfers (e.g. through regional policy)[13] are likely to be ineffective in encouraging sound long-term economic improvement; and, finally, that none of these considerations is likely to be relevant to the argument for and against fixed exchange rates, since the ability of poorer countries to improve their competitive position through devaluation of the currency is in any case extremely limited.

In all the arguments about the use of exchange-rate adjustments as an instrument of policy, it is important to recall that the EMU is only about exchange-rate stability *within* the EC. Together or separately, European currencies will continue to fluctuate against other currencies, notably the dollar and the yen. One issue for Britain is the likely effect on its trade denominated in these currencies of tying sterling effectively to the mark. Another, more political, consideration, is British involvement in any international discussion about greater world-wide exchange-rate stability. Here it must be clear that Britain's influence would be greater as part of a European monetary system than as an outsider.

Issues for the Intergovernmental Conference

What, then, are the main issues which will have to be resolved within the Community institutions or, in so far as they involve Treaty amendment, by the IGC? Much work has already been done by the Committee of Central Bank Governors and the Monetary Committee (with members drawn from national finance departments and central banks), and it is the aim of the Italian Presidency to present the IGC with a complete draft text at the start of its deliberations. Nevertheless, some important issues are likely to persist and may fall to Heads of Government to resolve in the European Council. These are: (a) whether to have fixed exchange rates or a single currency; (b) how to control the money supply; (c) what sort of Eurofed to set up; (d) how to control fiscal policy; and (e) how to get from where we are to where we want to be.

(a) Fixed exchange rates or a single currency?

Opinion seems to have swung decisively in favour of a single currency, rather than the retention of national currencies with irrevocably fixed exchange rates, though the Commission proposes a phased approach. If the markets could be convinced that rates were indeed permanently locked, the economic difference between the two proposals would be slight. However, a single currency would without doubt carry greater conviction that there could be no going back. On the other hand, in terms of public acceptability, the retention of national currencies might be preferred. One suggestion is that, if they so wished, member states could produce ecu notes and coins which would bear national insignia (e.g. the head of the Queen) on the reverse.

(b) The control of the money supply

It is generally accepted that price stability should be the top priority for any system, whether involving a single currency or permanently locked exchange rates. That in turn presupposes a central body with control over the money supply. In the words of the President of the Bundesbank, 'Without the monopoly of money creation the [Eurofed] would be a tiger without teeth.'[14] The question of how to achieve effective control over the money supply for the whole Community will require close technical study. At present, each country has its own measure or measures for the control of monetary aggregates (or in some cases none at all!). A common measure will probably be impracticable, but some degree of harmonization of national procedures will clearly be necessary for adequate control.

There appears to be widespread agreement that the powers of the Eurofed should not extend beyond control of the money supply into other areas of economic policy.

(c) What sort of Eurofed?

This is undoubtedly one of the most sensitive issues to be resolved and one which must feature in the Treaty if a final stage for EMU is to be agreed. The German position is unequivocal. The Eurofed should be the Bundesbank writ large: that is, a body appointed by governments but independent of further control by them and charged with the task of avoiding inflation. This form of central bank is built into the German constitution and endorsed by all the major political parties in the Federal Republic. The Bundesbank is widely credited with having achieved Germany's record of low inflation, but in fact at least as much credit should go to the German system of industrial relations and wage bargaining. In France, as in Britain, the central bank is under the direct control of the government, but the French government now appears ready to accept most of the German position.

In Britain, because of the reluctance to contemplate a European central bank in any form, the issue has been argued mainly in domestic terms. The majority view in parliament is plainly that the Bank of England should remain under the direct control of Treasury ministers and thus answerable, even if only indirectly, to Westminster. This view finds support on both sides of the political spectrum – from those on the left, who fear that an independent central bank would be insensitive to all policy considerations other than the control of inflation, and from those on the right, who put the importance of parliamentary control above even the likelihood that an independent central bank would be more successful in controlling inflation. The minority view, led by former Chancellor Nigel Lawson, regards the success of the German system in fighting inflation as so convincing that its supporters would settle for a lesser degree of parliamentary control and argue that, through procedures like allowing parliamentary committees to interrogate central bank officials, sufficient parliamentary accountability could be secured.

When transferred to the Community stage, the dilemma facing those who, like Mrs Thatcher, are staunch supporters of a tough anti-inflationary policy but are at the same time passionate defenders of the importance of the Westminster parliament is an acute one. Because of the opposition to the whole idea of a single currency, parliament has not yet faced up to the issue. There is irony in the prospect that the present British government, fearful that the Community would adopt lax monetary policies, might opt for an independent European central bank in preference to some political control, albeit at Community level. This would sit oddly with its concern about the importance of democratic control. Here, as elsewhere, judgment is clouded by the issue of Parliamentary sovereignty. It is a theme of this study that, once the decision has been taken to shift responsibility for policy to the Community level, the institutional consequences should follow without raising the issue of sovereignty afresh.

Unless the Germans are to have it all their own way, some constitutional ingenuity will have to be shown. The Commission has spoken of a mandate for the Eurofed which, while setting price stability as the overriding objective, would nevertheless charge it also with the task of supporting the general policy set by the Council. This could provide an opening. The Dutch system, which is close to that of the Bundesbank but gives the government reserve powers to direct the central bank in extreme circumstances (powers which in fact it has never formally exercised), might also offer the basis for compromise. The Treaty could give reserve powers of direction to the Council of Ministers while imposing on Eurofed the priority task of maintaining price stability.

(d) Fiscal policy

As mentioned earlier, there has been some retreat from the recommendations of the Delors Committee that the Community would need to lay down binding rules on the size of budget deficits in individual member states. It is now argued that the market would put sufficient pressure on a recalcitrant member state, provided two rules were observed: no monetary financing of budget deficits and no bailing out by the rest of the Community of a member state which gets into budgetary difficulty. To these, the Commission proposes adding consultative procedures which, it is thought, will achieve 'peer group pressure'. Whether such a set of measures will be sufficient to achieve budgetary convergence or, as others believe,[15] high borrowing countries will find ways to avoid the disciplines of the market must remain an open question. Given the political sensitivities, it seems likely that governments will be ready to take a chance.

(e) The route to EMU

The British plan for a 'hard' ecu, which would coexist with existing national currencies, demonstrates that there is more than one route leading from where the Community is today to the point at which it will have achieved full monetary union. There are basically three choices:

(a) concentrating on the existing EMS and making it more difficult for member states to adjust their rates so that eventually the currencies are permanently locked. This was basically the approach of the Delors Committee.

(b) building up the existing ecu – a 'basket' of the existing EMS currencies – so that it eventually becomes the only currency people want to hold or deal in. This is the approach advocated in the report commissioned for the Association for the Monetary Union of Europe.[16]

(c) creating at the outset a separate 'hard' ecu which, because it would hold its value better than any other, would progressively be preferred and thus be the obvious choice to become the single EC currency. This is the British proposal.

The political choice rests between (a) and (c). Supporters of the British proposal see the elements of choice and market evolution as virtues. They are seen as the recipe for the long haul. But the very indeterminateness of this approach is seen as a disadvantage by those who are keen to move quickly and who believe the Community progresses best through politically set targets (quite apart from the technical arguments for allowing the market to know in advance when the various steps will be taken[17]). The decision may turn on just how quickly, when it comes to the crunch, everyone is prepared to commit themselves to a single currency. This will be influenced by the stability or otherwise of the money markets at the time; by the lessons to be drawn from the July 1990 unification of the two currencies in Germany; and by whether events in the Middle East or elsewhere have created a general sense of caution. The initial enthusiasm for a rapid timetable has evaporated. Nevertheless, at the political level there is likely to be strong pressure for agreement on all the stages that will take the EC to EMU, even if no precise timetable is laid down for the progression to the third and final stage.

All this is likely to present serious problems for the British government. The majority may not opt for the hard ecu. They will certainly want a pledge on the final goal of a single currency and will probably wish to make detailed provision for it. The constitutional position of the Eurofed may prove more contentious than it now appears. It is clear that one of the advantages seen by the government for its approach is precisely that the pace can be set by the market, and the success or otherwise of economic and monetary policies in Europe. In this way difficult political decisions can be postponed. However, this does not seem to be possible. In the first place, unless the government is unequivocal about its commitment to the goal of EMU, it is not just future developments from which Britain risks being excluded, but the preparatory work on the whole design of the system. Thus, paradoxically, the chances of the pragmatic approach of the hard ecu finding support depends on a definite and early commitment by Britain to the final outcome. In the second place, the Community is likely to want to adopt the Treaty amendments which will put in place the European System of Central Banks and allow for a single European currency even if no timetable is laid down for its achievement. Britain will have to take a position. Once again, Britain's views on the terms and conditions for a move to the final stage will be relevant only if it is willing to sign up. If it refuses, the rest of the Community will go ahead.

Conclusion

There is no doubt that EMU has become today's talisman: the test of European virility and the token of Germany's commitment to the EC. Political enthusiasm may sweep aside expert hesitation. This could lead to disaster with serious consequences for the European economy and the cause of European integration. Or it could, as was the case with EMS, produce an achievement greater than the monetary pundits thought possible. There is room for genuine doubt as to whether the Community is really ready for full EMU. A speedy move to that end will undoubtedly make accession by the weaker economies of Eastern Europe more difficult. Most member states appear to have weighed up the arguments and are ready to take the plunge, if not rapidly at any rate within a reasonable time span.

On the other side, Britain remains divided. Industry and commerce largely share the view that 'a single market without a single currency is an expensive anachronism'[18] and that exclusion from a European system would be contrary to British interests. But the government is reluctant to accept the commitment to a single currency and the apparent loss of sovereignty which would be involved.[19] The dilemma is that Britain's legitimate arguments for a cautious approach will not be heeded if it is thought that the intention is to prevaricate rather than to ensure that the ultimate goal is reached in good order. It is therefore crucial for Britain to make it unequivocally clear that it too subscribes to the aim of a monetary union with a single currency, however long it may take to get there. It can then argue vigorously for its own preferred route while recognizing that the alternative may well carry the day. A compromise over the terms and conditions of the move to an eventual single currency should then be possible. Even a staggered timetable which left Britain (and perhaps other countries) with more time to adjust would be less damaging to long-term British interests than an arrangement which left Britain out until such time as it chose to join in.

Britain's influence within the Community has suffered from its prolonged absence from the ERM. To stay out of EMU would be to face accusations that once again Britain had missed the tide of European events. A treaty of which it was not a signatory is not what the rest of the Community wants. It could have serious consequences for Britain's role as the leading financial centre of Europe. The result might be not just a two-speed Europe but a two-class Europe.

7

REGIONAL AND SOCIAL ISSUES

'Tis not enough to help the feeble up,
'But to support him after'
— TIMON OF ATHENS

Will all in the race get prizes?

At each significant point in the recent development of the Community, whether it be enlargement, the EMS or the single market, one of the crucial issues has rightly been the impact on different regions. An initial tendency to assume that the creation of the EC would bring universal and uniform benefit (or perhaps an unwillingness to face up to the financial consequences of taking another view), gave way only slowly to the elaboration of a Community regional policy. Indeed, it was George Thomson, one of the first British Commissioners, who piloted through the first Regional Fund in 1975.

In its early stages, however, this Fund was much too small to have more than a marginal impact on the relative economic prosperity of the different regions of the Community; and even that was watered down in many countries, including Britain, by the practice of national finance ministries simply using Community money to replace rather than supplement what would otherwise have come from national funds. An eventual solution to the issue of 'additionality', plus increasingly effective lobbying by the poorer member states, significantly increased both the size of the Regional Fund and its influence in reducing regional disparities. The SEA gave treaty effect to the concept of 'economic and social cohesion' and included

69

the specific aim of 'reducing disparities between the various regions and the backwardness of the least-favoured regions'.

The most notable example of the growing power of the southern bloc of EC countries was the decision of the European Council in February 1988 that both the Regional and the Social Funds should double in real terms by 1993 as compared with 1987. The poorer member states, supported by the Commission, had argued that the benefits of the 1992 programme would not necessarily be universally and uniformly shared and that to achieve the greater economic and social cohesion of the Community required an increase in the transfers within the EC budget from the richer to the poorer member states.

Both the economic case and the financial cost were contested by the British government, but since the rest of the February 1988 package ensured a satisfactory containment of the British budget rebate and the introduction of financial controls on the CAP – both major British objectives – it accepted the demands of the southern bloc. It seems probable that similar demands will be made in connection with EMU, but this time a much tougher attitude from Britain seems likely, given its dislike of EMU and the absence of any countervailing objective that Britain will want to secure.

The fact is that the size of the Community budget is only a very modest element in the distribution of wealth within the Community. The 1988 agreement will lead to a slight increase in the Community budget, but even by 1992 it is scheduled to be less than 1.2% of Community GNP.[1] Nevertheless, as the debate over the British budget contribution demonstrated all too clearly, the methods of revenue gathering and allocation of expenditure do produce a redistributive effect which may be considered unfair (as it manifestly was in Britain's case) or justified (as in the case of Ireland, whose net receipts from the Community budget run at over 5% of GDP), but which is essentially haphazard. One of the major issues left unresolved in the European Council decisions of 1988 is whether the Community budget should set out to be deliberately redistributive and, if so, how.[2]

This issue was first ventilated in a systematic way by the study group set up by the Commission in 1977 and chaired by Sir Donald MacDougall.[3] In their report the group argued that to be capable of having a redistributive function comparable to that of the federal budgets of countries like Canada, the Community budget would need to be something like 7% of Community GDP. Even that would reduce regional inequalities within the EC by only about 40%. The issue of regional imbalances was analysed more recently in the Padoa-Schioppa report, another document commissioned by the EC Commission to study some of the macroeconomic issues facing the Community.[4] It endorsed the view that regional imbalances within the EC were a problem and that a redistributively designed EC budget was desirable.

The figures contained in that report are very telling – and there is no reason to suppose that more up-to-date figures would alter the picture substantially. GDP per head ranged from 43% of the EC average in the Greek region of Thrace to 237% of the average in Groningen, Netherlands. Unemployment rates at that time varied from 30% in Andalucia in Spain to under 5% in several of the German Länder.

In recent years, the problems of regional development have been given considerable attention. The Commission, in a series of initiatives, has sought to develop a more integrated approach to the agricultural, industrial, economic and social needs of the most disadvantaged areas of the Community. It will be some time before it is possible to assess the long-term benefits of these measures. The major developments which are taking place within the Community and the prospect, however distant, of further enlargement to include economies which are even less developed than those of, say, Greece and Portugal, provide a good case for having yet another major study of the whole issue of regional development and its implications for the Community budget and other policies. What has been the impact on regional disparities of the structural funds so far distributed by the EC? What should be done about member states which cannot or do not find the national funds required to 'match' the EC contributions? Do transfers have to be conditional? What would a redistributive budget look like and how would it work? Since major new decisions on the Community budget will need to be taken by about 1992, as was discussed in Chapter 5, the results of such an inquiry would be very valuable.[5]

Because of the present British government's antipathy to public expenditure in general and Community expenditure in particular, the question whether this country would gain or lose from the development of a purposely designed Community budget, in which the transfers between member states bore some rational relationship to need and the ability to pay, has not been given much serious attention. The case for a redistributive budget has been espoused by the new pro-European elements in the Labour Party, but again without the implications for Britain appearing to have been thought through.

It was always part of Britain's argument in favour of an adjustment of its net contribution to the EC budget that it was inequitable for a country with a GDP per head somewhere around the Community average to find itself making the largest net contribution after Germany. However, the case was never built solely or even largely on redistributive grounds precisely because of the fear that this would appear to endorse the policy of large transfers in favour of the poorest member states and thus act against Britain's long-term interests. As Table 1 (in Chapter 2) has shown, Britain's GDP per head remains close to the EC average. On the face of it, therefore, Britain should end up somewhere near all square in such a redistributive budget. But there is room here for some serious academic work.

The social partners
The Treaty of Rome sections dealing with social matters (Articles 117–22) contained only one requirement to have a common policy. It dealt with equal pay and was inserted, it is claimed, less in the interests of promoting the cause of equality for women than because the French government had just introduced equal pay and did not want to be undercut by cheap female labour from other member states. As we shall see, this tension between the wish to avoid distortion of competition and the desire to pursue social policy objectives still runs through the debate on what is known as the Community's 'social dimension'.

The Single European Act added one other article, providing for the adoption (by qualified majority) of directives dealing with the health and safety of workers, again with the elimination of unfair competition as one of the main considerations. It is true that during the 1970s and early 1980s some highly contentious efforts were made to include provisions on worker participation in European company law; but very little was achieved, partly because of the need to rely on unanimity and partly because the Commission was then still attached to the concept of harmonization throughout the Community. It was not until the impetus of the single market and the recognition that the harmonization route was not the only possible one that anything like a coherent social policy began to emerge.[6] Both the Commission and the European Parliament felt concerned that the benefits to be expected from the single market programme might not be equally shared by workers as well as businesses. This led to the Social Charter, adopted at the Strasbourg European Council in December 1989 by eleven of the twelve Heads of Government.

The British Prime Minister declined to go along with the rest, believing that the Charter was misconceived and put at risk her government's policies of reducing the powers of the trade unions and tackling unemployment by getting rid of unnecessary regulation. This rejection of the Charter attracted considerable criticism from the Opposition, the TUC and the public. By her refusal, however, Mrs Thatcher avoided any political commitment to the Social Action Programme which the Commission brought forward to give effect to the intentions of the Charter. Other member states, which may have had similar reservations, decided that they could live with the rhetoric and still resist the detail.

Some of the Commission's views may indeed be rather backward-looking and take insufficient account of the more progressive thinking about how to handle industrial relationships in the 1990s. Just as the 1985 programme for the single market contained many items which had been around for a long time, the Social Action Programme contains many proposals which were first put forward in the 1960s and 1970s. At that time they had fallen on stony ground and 'here, in the Action Programme, one after another, like ghosts from Councils past, they emerge from their troubled oblivion'.[7]

Following the Prime Minister's refusal to accept the Social Charter, the government's reaction to the Social Action Programme has been mixed. According to the Department of Employment, only about a third of the 47 or so measures envisaged by the Commission are likely to cause fundamental difficulty for Britain, another third are too vague and unclear to say whether they will be acceptable or not and the remaining third are likely to be acceptable subject to detailed negotiation. The objections turn on whether it is necessary to have Community intervention in employment law and whether statutory measures are necessary at all, or will be unduly burdensome on employers.

There has been particularly strong opposition to the proposed regulation of part-time and temporary working. The goverment's argument (endorsed by both British and EC employers' organizations) is that the current freedom enjoyed by employers in the use of part-time and temporary workers increases employment and the ability to compete on world markets. The counter-argument is that part-time workers may compete for jobs unfairly if they are not subject to the same requirements as full-time workers. In Britain, for example, part-time workers who earn less than a certain threshold are exempt from both employee and employer contributions towards the cost of National Insurance. As regards job creation, it can be asked whether the argument is one that can be applied to part-time working alone. If the absence of regulation is necessary for greater competitiveness and the freedom for employers and employees to negotiate their own conditions of work will reduce unemployment, then that consideration is likely to apply with at least equal force to full-time employment. And if the concessions to part-time workers improve their ability to compete on world markets, will they not also improve the competitive position of British industry within the single market?

The British government may be on good grounds in arguing that some matters affecting conditions of work, which have traditionally been the subject of legislation, can in fact be safely left to the free play of the market or the voluntary agreement of management and labour. There is room here for genuine argument, either at national or at EC level. There is very little doubt, for example, that if EC-wide minimum requirements are set too high, the competitive advantage which the poorer, low-wage regions of the Community have (and need) will be eroded – with adverse consequences for their ability to achieve the necessary economic growth.

Where the government appears to be on less firm ground is in its assertion that effective action is being taken at the level of the member states and should be left there. This appeal to the subsidiarity principle must rest either on the argument that national action is already reasonably harmonized or on the argument that, where it is not, the distortion of competition between one member state and another is minimal (which appears to be the basis of the employers' stance on temporary and part-time working). The government's case appears to be that health and safety is the only area where there would be unfair competition, unless regulation is on a Community-wide basis. But, once again, it seems more convincing to claim that the matter does not require regulation at all, whether at national or at Community level, than that, if the case for regulation is made out, some degree of harmonization for the EC as a whole is unnecessary. Perhaps the reluctance to admit the argument reflects an appreciation of the consequence: namely, that if the weight of Community opinion is in favour of regulation, Britain would logically have to rally to the majority view.

Employers in Britain have supported the government's efforts to avoid unnecessary regulation in this field but they have been more ready to embrace the concept of a social dimension for the EC.[8] In particular, employers do not at all reject the idea of an appropriate dialogue between the social partners. The attitude of the British trade union movement towards dialogue is also positive. Here too some emphasis is placed on the scope for cooperation rather than confrontation:

> The choice that is open to the Community is two-fold. Either we can export the British system of industrial relations to Europe, with its institutionalized conflict, or we can import the European mode of working together to get the best of our industry. If the Single European Market can institutionalize competition among companies, there should be no reason why it cannot institutionalize co-operation between the managers and employers who work in them.'[9]

While there is readiness on both sides to cooperate and to engage in dialogue, it must be recognized that there is strong resistance to accepting that the trade unions have any monopoly in the protection and representation of worker interests. The Institute of Directors has been prominent in arguing that the current approach of the Commission still shows undue emphasis on the role of organized labour and does not sufficiently address itself to the rights of the individual worker. This criticism has been heard most forcibly in Britain, but it has also been taken up by industrial leaders elsewhere in the EC and by the European employers' organization UNICE.[10]

If the fear of undue government interference in the regulation of the market characterizes the employers' approach to 'Social Europe', the concern of workers is that the burden of adjustment which will undoubtedly result from the 1992 programme will fall on them and that, with freer movement, they will face unfair competition from workers with lower standards – a concern which is widespread not only in Britain but among the more prosperous member states, and known as 'social dumping'. The term is most commonly used to mean the fear that the opening up of the single market will cause investment to shift to the poorer countries of the Community where wages are low, and that either jobs in the more prosperous countries will be lost or 'there will be overwhelming pressures on working people to limit their wage demands and accept lower conditions in order to maintain a competitive advantage'.[11] But as the same document recognizes, 'the post-1992 economic situation conjured up by the spectre of social dumping fails to take account of the influence of productivity as a factor in industrial planning. Differences in productivity sharply narrow the scope for social dumping.' To the extent that this is true – and the former territory of East Germany will be an immediate and vivid test of whether the much lower productivity there will be reflected in lower wages – the unit labour costs may not be so very different. If, however, lower productivity is *not* reflected in lower wages, very little private investment will find its way to places like East Germany, and unemployment there will rise.

Migrant workers
If there are concerns about the social costs of the 1992 internal market programme, there are equally worries about the external threat. During the years of rapid growth and labour shortages, most EC countries came to rely on immigrant labour. This was absorbed without too much friction because demand was strong, and almost certainly made a positive contribution to growth and to wealth in the EC. But with the increase in unemployment, tensions have heightened. With some 3.6 million immigrants (chiefly from North Africa), now accounting for some 6.5% of the total population, France has already experienced several racial incidents, and the rise of the extreme right owes much to its racist policies. The same is true of West Germany, where the traditional immigrant workers from Turkey and the Mediterranean area now in turn face competition from the former East Germany and the bordering newly democratic states. Concern is also mounting in Italy, where over three-quarters of the estimated 1.3m immigrants have arrived illegally.

But North Africa faces a population explosion. The present population of working age (i.e. between the ages of 15 and 64) is currently estimated to be about 67 million. That number is expected to rise to 106 million by the year 2000 and to 178 million in 2025. Such a massive increase in the number of job seekers presents the EC with one of its greatest and most difficult challenges. It could well be exacerbated if the Soviet Union eases up on its own exit visa policy. Given the ageing population in the EC and the increasing reluctance of many to do unskilled manual work, there will continue to be a demand, and perhaps even a growing demand, for 'guest workers'. But it cannot match the explosion in the potential supply. The EC governments, already facing huge racial, ethnic and social difficulties, are likely to see the problem as a serious potential threat to social stability. The treatment of migrant workers within the Community has long been a source of concern[12] and will need greater attention alongside the case for tighter controls on illegal immigration from outside the EC. The reluctance of the Schengen countries (see Chapter 5) to accept Italy into the club arose principally from doubt about its ability to control immigration.

Immigration policy, currently the jealously guarded preserve of national governments, is another example of the inevitable consequences of the 1992 programme. Fewer border controls, coupled with the pressure of external events, will force governments into much closer coordination of their national policies. Even if there is no formal transfer of competence, what each country does will need to fit into some coherent Community strategy. This is already beginning to happen not only with immigration policy but in the handling of related issues like visas. As discussed in Chapter 5, the freer the movement at the border the greater the need for coordination of procedures, and eventually of policies.

The adoption by the Community of a more defensive policy designed to curb the flow of immigrants from the south will add a new dimension and a new urgency to the Community's existing and uneasy links with the Mediterranean area which were discussed in Chapter 3. One of the understandable concerns of the Mediterranean countries (EC members and non-members alike) is that monies – both public and private – which might otherwise have come to assist their economic development will be diverted to the newly democratic countries of Eastern Europe, which have closer racial, cultural and religious ties with the West. These fears are shared by labour throughout the Community. Whether the immigrants come from the east or the south they are seen as potential competitors – if not taking jobs then forcing down wages. Whether the capital investment is diverted to Eastern Europe or to North Africa, it is seen as a potential loss of employment opportunities within the Community. These fears are doubtless misplaced. They fail to take account of the demographic changes inside the EC or of the job-creating impact of economic growth. Nevertheless they are still a potent political factor – as much in Britain as in other EC countries, even though Britain's geographical position means that it is not in the front line of these potential immigration pressures.

The British attitude

For ideological reasons, the present British government has tended to dismiss the argument for social cohesion and related aspects of the Community. But these are issues to which a large section of the population – in Britain as throughout the Community – attaches importance. A modest but growing part of the EC budget goes to the regional, social and structural funds. At its best, the Community is encouraging constructive collaboration at EC, national and, especially, local level to develop the poorer regions. At its worst, Community money is being wasted or even fraudulently misapplied. The latter will need to be remedied. It seems unlikely that the regional disparities within the existing Community will disappear of their own accord; moreover, if the Community is enlarged, the need for coordinated Community action will increase. These and other developments over the next few years are likely to present the EC with some potentially explosive social situations. They will not be easy to handle. Competences are shared between the EC and the member states and likely to remain so; traditions are strong and national perceptions acutely different.

The differences are historical, ideological and cultural, as well as reflecting the two sides of industry. For instance, the TUC has made great efforts to get alongside its French counterparts. It has found that there are important differences in legal traditions, in negotiating techniques and in the structure of unions. This has not prevented fruitful collaboration on EC issues but it illustrates why the attempts to define a European social policy have often seemed ineffectual and to have generated more heat than light. This has been exacerbated in

Britain by the radical shift in policies and attitudes since the Conservatives came to power in 1979. It is hardly surprising that the New Right does not want to see its gains eroded by what is perceived as a still corporatist EC, even if there have been some notable political shifts, especially in France. It is equally unsurprising that the Labour Party and the TUC have shown considerable enthusiasm for the Social Charter and its Action Programme. That there should be an ideological debate between left and right is entirely understandable and that it should be increasingly conducted on a European as well as a national level reflects the shifting focus. On both sides, the relevant British organizations are making a significant contribution to the industrial debate, which transcends nationality.

To many British and other multinational companies, much of the debate must seem unreal, since in practice they are having to cope with and no doubt exploit the different national characteristics and regulations with which they have to operate. The lesson of their experience appears to be that market processes may be more effective than legislation in bringing about desirable change. A study commissioned by Unilever concluded that consultation with the workforce was carried out as effectively on a voluntary basis in Britain as in the Netherlands and Germany, where there are elaborate regulations about consultation.

There is a belief in Britain that Germany aims to export its elaborate system of statutory worker participation in large firms to the rest of the Community just to ensure that German industry is not at a competitive disadvantage. Another view is that German employers would like to be shot of their system but are prevented from doing so by the politicians. There is not a great deal of evidence for either view. In any event, the latest proposals (e.g. for a European company statute) do not oblige countries to take up the German system.   _

Just as many of the large employers in Germany genuinely believe that they have found a winning formula which they do not wish to abandon for something inferior, so are many people in Britain equally convinced that their own government's voluntary and deregulatory approach is best. The right course is to seek to convince the rest of the Community of the strength of the British argument. There are without doubt many others in the Community who share the view that regulation can sometimes be anti-competitive and anti-employment. The aim must be to agree on what is 'best practice' in each case: not to insist on absolute uniformity but to recognize that there is as good a case for a reasonably level playing-field in the regulation of industrial relations and perhaps other social policies as there is, for instance, in the regulation of mergers and takeovers.

As regards the Social Action Programme, the right course must be to examine each of the proposals on its merits. The test which the British government has proposed – do the proposals lead to the creation of jobs? – is a perfectly valid one, though there may be others.[13] Britain is on weaker ground, however, in seeking to push the Community out of the argument.

8

A GREEN EUROPE

'Fair is foul and foul is fair,
'Hover through the fog and filthy air'
— MACBETH

With the growing awareness of environmental problems over recent years, and an increasing ambition among state leaders and public opinion alike to do something about it, it is hardly surprising that environmental policy has become a growth industry in the EC. The year 1992 has significance not only as the target-date for the single market but also as the twentieth anniversary of the Stockholm Conference which first focused attention on the world's major environmental problems. The two events are not unconnected. It was the Brundtland Report of 1987 which concluded that economic growth *could* be reconciled with environmental imperatives, but only on certain well-defined conditions.[1] Stricter environmental standards were essential for sustainable development. The EC can be said to have accepted the logic of that conclusion. At its meeting in December 1988, the European Council declared that 'the industrial and competitive future of Europe on the world market partly depends on the application of [a] high level of environmental protection'.

The European Community's environmental policy, launched in 1972 following the Stockholm Conference, was developed through a series of Environmental Action Programmes. The first two concentrated on trying to remedy the most obvious pollution problems.

The third programme, adopted in 1983, shifted the emphasis from cure to prevention. By the time of the Intergovernmental Conference which led to the Single European Act, it was clear that environmental issues had become central to many of the Community's policies. Governmental pressure from the more environmentally conscious member states, such as the Netherlands, Germany and Denmark, gave backing to the Commission and led to the inclusion, for the first time, of specific environmental obligations in the Treaties. These provisions contained a number of significant features.

First, the Act not only spells out the objectives of Community environmental policy but seeks to integrate them into the Community's other policies. Because of the range of its functions, the EC is uniquely well placed to achieve this combination of environmental and economic policy-making. The horizontal integration of environmental objectives through the requirement that environmental protection must be a component of other Community policies should strengthen the relevant Directorate General (DG XI) in relation to other Commission services.[2]

Second, the principle that the 'polluter pays' is firmly written into the provisions of the Act, thus ruling out subsidization and, hopefully, market distortion. Third, the Act provides for the possible use of qualified majority voting, and the Council has now agreed that this can apply to the setting of environmental standards, though no such decisions have yet been taken. It is thus too early to judge what impact majority voting will have on the environmental programme. Nevertheless, there is already some frustration in the European Parliament and elsewhere that, whereas certain environmental issues are automatically subject to majority voting by using Article 100A, the new Article 130S still requires a unanimous decision to extend majority voting to other environmental cases. As discussed in Chapter 9, this will certainly lead to pressure for further amendment in the forthcoming Intergovernmental Conference on institutional matters.

Finally, the environmental provisions of the SEA are interesting from a constitutional point of view because they make explicit reference to the principle of subsidiarity.[3] It is too early to say just how the principle will work out in practice, and certainly too early to draw any conclusions which might be relevant in other areas. One

Table 3   EC reductions in sulphur dioxide emissions

		Emission ceilings			% reduction over 1980		
	Emissions 1980	1993	1998	2003	1993	1998	2003
		(thousand tonnes/year)					
Belgium	530	318	212	159	−40	−60	−70
Denmark	323	213	141	106	−34	−56	−67
Germany	2225	1335	890	668	−40	−60	−70
Greece	303	320	320	320	+6	+6	+6
Spain	2290	2290	1730	1440	0	−24	−37
France	1910	1146	764	573	−40	−60	−70
Ireland	99	124	124	124	+25	+25	+25
Italy	2450	1800	1500	900	−27	−39	−63
Luxembourg	3	1.8	1.5	1.5	−40	−50	−60
Netherlands	299	180	120	90	−40	−60	−70
Portugal	115	232	270	206	+102	+135	+79
UK	3883	3106	2330	1553	−20	−40	−60
EC	**14430**	**11065**	**8402**	**6140**	**−23**	**−42**	**−58**

Source: RSA Journal, vol. CXXXVII, no. 5396 (July 1989).

application of the principle which undoubtedly has its place in environmental policy is the setting of goals at the EC level while leaving discretion over means to the member states. A notable case where this technique has already been used is in the so-called Large Combustion Plant Directive, which lays down requirements for the gradual reduction in sulphur dioxide emissions up to the year 2003 – with the additional, highly dubious, novelty of setting different targets for different member states (see Table 3). Nevertheless, the evolution and growing weight of Community legislation does suggest – not surprisingly – that governmental action will increasingly be at Community rather than national level. It may be premature to conclude, as the Institute for European Environmental Policy has done, that 'for environmental purposes the European Community is now a federal system',[4] but it is undoubtedly the case that the Community has achieved a great deal in applying environmental principles and far more than could have been achieved in any other way. It justifies the claim that 'the creation of a common policy on the environment has been one of the Community's great triumphs, though it has gone largely unrecognised'.[5]

A changing British stance

Britain's reputation as 'the dirty man of Europe' is largely based on one aspect of environmental pollution – the volume of sulphur dioxide and nitrogen oxide emissions which, because of the nature of the British power industry, substantially exceed those of other EC countries. But as regards environmental policy, Britain's reputation varies. The British are widely acknowledged to have been pioneers in nature conservation, town and country planning and even clean air legislation. On the other hand, the British government's reluctance to admit to any collective responsibility, notably for the effects of acid rain, created much resentment. The Community's first Environmental Action Programme (1973) was dismissed by Britain as excessively costly, insufficiently well-founded on scientific evidence, and likely to be disadvantageous to British industry and to economic growth. Britain's situation was seen as being different from that of other Community member states. Internal arrangements were preferred to more interventionist Community action. Much scepticism was shown on the value of fixing environmental standards, and even more towards harmonization as a means to achieve environmental ends. All these arguments, in the view of one observer, 'served to leave the UK for long periods in an isolated minority of one in debate after debate in the Environment Council'.[6]

In the last few years, partly under pressure from public opinion, partly because of the evident fact that, whether Britain liked it or not, the EC was going to be the scene for much action on the environmental front, and partly from the realization that EC standards were highly desirable on competitive grounds, the British position has changed. In the first place, the environment has been accorded a higher profile in the government's policy, as signalled by the Prime Minister's speech on the environment to the Royal Society in September 1988. That shift in policy allowed the government to take a more positive role in the Brussels negotiations. As a result, it has in fact agreed with its Community partners on the adoption of a large and important body of Community legislation, and the Commission's original proposals were often modified to meet British concerns. The Large Combustion Plant Directive, already referred to, was one such decision, taken in November 1988 after six years of complex and tedious negotiation (with Britain eventually accepting percentage reductions roughly equal to the average for the EC as a whole, as shown in Table 3).

More recently still, the change in government policy was reinforced by a change in style with the departure of Nicholas Ridley and the arrival of Chris Patten as Secretary of State for the Environment. Instead of appearing to view the activities of the EC with reluctance, the new Secretary of State set about inculcating a more positive attitude and a sense of more willing participation. This has been welcomed by the rest of the Community. It is a good illustration of how a change in style, even without a change in substance, can make others more ready to listen to British arguments and thus enhance the chances of British views prevailing.

This improved atmosphere is likely to be of some importance as the environmental story unfolds both in Britain and within the Community. In Britain, awareness of the costs involved in reaching the agreed standards (£2 billion for the flue gas desulphurization programme to comply with the Large Plant Directive alone) has led to some dampening of enthusiasm for the environment and even some back-tracking. This is reflected in the government's White Paper on the Environment. Its contents were no doubt drawn up with the general election casting its shadow forward, but the Department of the Environment does not appear to have strengthened its hand in its customary battles with other Whitehall departments.

In one case – the water industry – the struggle has been an internal one. The Department of the Environment was responsible for the privatization of the water industry as well as for ensuring proper standards of cleanliness in the water supply. Having agreed in 1980 to the Drinking Water Directive, the government found that the Commission's interpretation of the Directive meant the requirements laid down could not be met and, furthermore, that any forcing of the pace on compliance would prejudice the chances of successful privatization of the industry. The issue was resolved only after threats of court action and some torrid negotiations with the Commission. As with the comparable issue of sulphur dioxide emissions and its implications for the privatization of the electricity supply industry, the conflicting interests within the British government were mirrored in the corresponding directorates of the European Commission, but in the Commission's case the balance of forces seems to be firmly in favour of the environment. Because it does not carry responsibility for the costs and inconveniences involved in implementing policy, the Commission can be accused of paying insufficient regard to this aspect, and in some cases (the response to the Chernobyl disaster and the setting of standards for nitrates in water are two examples) it appears to have gone beyond the best scientific evidence in response to public pressure. But as regards the episode of the Drinking Water Directive, there is no doubt that public opinion in Britain sided with the Commission in its efforts to enforce acceptable standards of water quality and did not take kindly to the government's delaying tactics.

The programme

In Brussels, important new initiatives are under discussion. The most controversial revolve around the concept of an energy or carbon tax and the harmonization of duty on fuels. The case for improved energy efficiency and saving is overwhelming and in Britain, as in the other member states, there is scope for more to be done. Taxing energy use would undoubtedly contribute to this objective and is consistent with the principle that the polluter pays; but it raises highly sensitive political issues which will make governments hesitate. The sudden rise in energy prices as a result of the Gulf crisis, while strengthening the case for improved efficiency, will add to these hesitations. In Britain, any increase in petrol prices is unwelcome in the struggle to bring down inflation, and higher costs will be bitterly opposed by the transport and automobile industries. However, the Dutch National Environmental Policy Plan (NEPP) already contains the idea of a domestic carbon tax, the proceeds of which will be used to finance other environmental measures. Plainly, there is a strong case on competitive grounds as well as on grounds of effectiveness for the EC to move as a whole, and Britain should look more carefully at the Commission's ideas or come up with an equally effective alternative.

The Commission's suggestion for an environmental audit of companies also has interesting possibilities. The outcome may be a framework law obliging EC companies to carry out and publish environmental audits. This could be seen as imposing yet another administrative burden on industry. On the other hand, the result could be positive, with companies competing for the best environmental record in response to an increasingly critical public scrutiny.

The Commission has also proposed a Waste Damage Directive to provide protection for people affected by pollution of water, soil or air as a result of the handling of waste. Those suffering damage to health or property would be able to make a legal claim against the person or company whose activities were the cause of the environmental damage, whether in the initial production of the waste or in its subsequent disposal. There are obvious legal and practical problems in this proposal but it is an interesting extension of the 'polluter pays' principle.

The means

Three issues of importance to Britain concern the way environmental problems are dealt with. The first is the way in which the 'polluter pays' principle is applied in practice. The most straightforward route is the regulatory one: the law restricts what the potential polluter can do and requires him to bear whatever is the cost of compliance. Many in industry prefer this route because it guarantees fair competition, gives a greater sense of certainty and can provide the initial incentive to adopting a positive environmental posture. But it is not favoured by the present British government with its strong antipathy towards regulation – and especially regulation from Brussels.

The alternative approach makes use of economic instruments to influence decisions in an environmentally friendly direction. To the British government there are obvious attractions in using methods which, once the ground rules have been laid, allow the market to reconcile the interests of economic growth and environmental protection. But the government is very cautious about anything which smacks of harmonization. Thus, while the tax differential in favour of unleaded petrol is widely quoted as an excellent British initiative, the government shows no wish to impose the same fiscal system on the rest of the Community. Britain has also been innovative in the use of financial incentives in the management of environmentally sensitive farming areas, and these ideas have been taken up by the Community. The Dutch NEPP contains a range of financial incentives such as tax allowances for commuting costs, tolls at key traffic points and peak-hour surcharges on motor vehicle taxes. It is to be hoped that, in spite of its reservations, the British government will come forward with its own suggestions for sensible ways in which EC environmental objectives can be set and achieved.

The second issue, the pressure to extend the use of majority voting to all environmental issues – supported by the Labour Party – will present the British government with a dilemma. It will not wish to appear unenthusiastic about achieving the more rapid progress towards generally applicable EC environmental standards which majority voting would permit. On the other hand, apart from the general sovereignty issue, it will be afraid of being forced to go further than British economic interests might warrant. It will certainly argue that where fiscal policy is involved, as with a carbon tax, unanimity must be maintained. This, of course, need not rule out the British government agreeing to such a tax, but if all fiscal methods of dealing with the environment are made subject to unanimity the result may be either that progress is slower than one would wish or that other, perhaps less desirable, methods have to be used. Moreover, British success in persuading its Community partners that VAT harmonization was not essential to the single market (see Chapter 5) ought not to set a precedent for environmental policy – where the case for EC harmonization is stronger. Thus Britain should give its agreement to majority voting on all environmental issues, including fiscal measures specific to the environment, but it might seek to make that agreement conditional on strong measures being taken to ensure compliance with standards which have been agreed.

The question of enforcement leads on to the third issue, another novelty in EC environmental policy: the creation of a separate European Environmental Agency (EEA). Recognizing that its own resources were limited and that it needed a source of independent scientific advice, the Commission proposed the creation of this semi-autonomous body, which would collect, evaluate and disseminate EC environmental data. Agreed in principle, the functions of the EEA are due to be decided by March 1992. Britain, keen on seeing scientific proof in environmental analysis, has given full support to the Agency. The EEA could well serve as a 'pro-enforcement' body, advising the Commission or acting as a bridge between the Commission and the European Court of Justice; and there are those who would go further and give the Agency independent powers of enforcement, by analogy with similar agencies in some member states (including Britain). The regulation setting up the EEA provides for the possibility of extending membership to third countries. Both the East European countries (whose environmental problems are immense) and EFTA have shown interest in joining the collaborative action of the EEA, and the advantages from an environmental point of view are obvious. But the debate on this issue – as on the enforcement role of the EEA – will be watched with great interest also by those who see the whole concept of agencies as another valuable innovation in the EC's institutional structure.[7]

Conclusion

In most of the key environmental problems of the 1990s – safe and sustainable energy supplies; the greenhouse effect and other climatic changes; the preservation of forests; environmentally acceptable agricultural practices; the protection of genetic resources and the management of waste – it is clear that the EC will be a major player. On the global issues, the EC will have to press for global solutions and must decide whether, until they are possible, it will act unilaterally or with such partners as it can find. The Community should not be afraid to use its economic muscle to make help to third countries, whether in Eastern Europe or in the Third World, conditional upon improvement in environmental standards.

Within Europe, increasingly demanding standards appear to be unavoidable and will present difficult choices for British as for other governments. Where Britain is lagging behind (and energy efficiency is one such case), it will have to accept the short-term costs involved in catching up. Where it is ahead, it will want to see strict enforcement of the obligations on those who have to catch up.

Britain has much to contribute. It has technical expertise and research capabilities which are widely respected. It has a powerful, well-informed and generally responsible environmental lobby. It has been innovative in many environmental areas. Thus it is all the more unfortunate that the British government has so often instinctively reacted against EC proposals even when it has eventually gone along with them. The approach of reservation and reluctance did not pay off and fortunately has now been abandoned. There will inevitably be difficult choices to be made in reconciling the interests of the ecology, current and future consumers, industry and the taxpayer; but in most of these the arguments in Britain will not be substantially different from those in other EC countries. It now appears to have been accepted that the extent to which environmental problems cross boundaries makes the case for action on at least EC level irrefutable. There will continue to be problems in agreeing on what can best be done at the Community level and what is best left to the discretion of individual member states (the subsidiarity principle), but objectively the choice should not be too difficult. With so much more still to do, there will be an interesting political interplay between those areas where Britain can help to push the rest of the EC in the right direction and those where the opposite will be true. This still leaves plenty of scope for Britain to play the leading role in the development of environmental policies which will be both in its own interest and in the interest of the Community as a whole.

9
DEMOCRATIC CONTROL AND INSTITUTIONAL REFORM

> 'O, it is excellent
> 'To have a giant's strength, but it is tyrannous
> 'To use it like a giant'
> – MEASURE FOR MEASURE

Introduction

Two points are crucial for the British debate about the Community institutions. The first is to recognize that a transfer of responsibility from the national to the Community level does not necessarily involve more 'state control' of the economy or of the individual. The quantum of government intervention is increased only if the policies being pursued at the Community level are more *dirigiste* than those at the national level, or if the national authorities insist on continuing to regulate as well. In practice, that can happen, and this is the fear of many over the Social Action Programme. In principle, the 'frontiers of the state' can be set at whatever point the controlling authority decides. That is a matter of political choice, at the Community level as at the national one. At present, Britain's reluctance to see matters dealt with at the Community level often seems due more to the fear that the British government's view about where the frontier should lie will not be shared by the rest of the Community, than to the intrinsic merits of the argument about what the right level should be.

The second point to stress is that for the foreseeable future, and probably for all time, the EC will consist of a unique combination of member states and transnational Community institutions, with features unprecedented in the literature of political science. What is

91

emerging in Europe is not likely to be a centralized system of government. Indeed, it is rare for federal systems to develop dominant institutions at the centre. When compared with other international organizations, the EC looks like a system of strong government. However, the EC was never intended to be just another international organization but an explicit agreement by independent states 'to pool and share their sovereignty in clearly defined spheres of activity'.[1]

Thus the whole institutional framework of the European Community in place today relies on the notion that, despite different political and cultural traditions and ideologies, member states can practise collective decision-making. Coalition-building plays a key role in this. As both Community policies and institutions have grown and expanded, they have left their mark on the Community's 'democratic model'. Nevertheless it remains, as it was initially drawn, a fundamentally 'continental' model, shaped largely by its founding members and their practices. As discussed in Chapter 2, that tradition operates through 'a process of give-and-take in which no single party or social interest can expect to get all it wants, but in which all or nearly all have some influence on the outcome'.[2]

The English model of government, on the other hand, relies on offering the electorate the periodic choice between alternative governments with distinct political persuasions. The contrast between the Community model and the Westminster model of government accounts for many of the particular worries and interests of British parliamentarians,[3] but it is not necessarily a good guide to the best way of improving the institutional arrangements in the European Community as they are.

What democratic deficit?
The contrast in approach is highly relevant to the debate over the so-called 'democratic deficit'. This is variously seen as stemming from the lack of accountability in EC decision-making, the weakness of political representation and the disequilibrium between Community and national institutions. All of these factors affect the legitimacy of European legislation. But the weight given to them depends on the political experience of each member state. Thus the British could judge the Community's model of coalition and consensus-building as both lacking accountability and too open to the pressures of

vested interests. Yet elsewhere in the EC, the British model of government is often viewed as undemocratic to the extent that it is exclusive and does not represent all political streams in society. Since it is the EC model which is under the microscope, however, criticism of its inadequacies must relate to that model and not to the national, British one.

The notion that the EC suffers from a democratic deficit is not new. It used to be addressed mainly in terms of a debate about the powers of the European Parliament. That debate continues, but is now flanked by a more general concern over accountability. This takes two forms: first, that the decisions of *all* the EC institutions (i.e. the Commission as well as the Council) need to be subjected to closer democratic scrutiny; and, second, that national parliaments should be enabled to make a more effective input into Community decision-making. Both aspects are seen as important in Britain (and recently in France too), but there is less concern with the second in some other member states.

In Britain, informed opinion ranges from those who think the problem of the democratic deficit is one of the biggest issues facing the EC to those who doubt whether, taking the Community model as a starting-point, much of a deficit exists at all. Others suspect that the issue has been exaggerated by those wishing merely to enhance the role of the European Parliament. It may also be exaggerated by those who regard Westminster as the only legitimate or effective source of democratic control. The conclusion of one expert is that, because the Council (and its many subsidiary bodies) remains, even after the SEA, the principal legislative body, 'by the consensus model's own criteria ... there *is* a democratic deficit, and it is likely to get bigger as the Community's functions expand'.[4]

What might be done about it, in relation to both the Council and the Commission, is addressed in the following sections along with the other considerations relating to institutional reform. It will not be easy to find solutions, given the range of opinion about the nature of the problem. It is difficult to imagine, however, any starting-point other than a continuation of the consensus model. The proposals for institutional reform that are likely to find favour at the Inter-governmental Conference will build on, not replace, the existing framework.

Reform of the Community's institutions is again high on the political agenda, and rightly so. Given the expanding tasks and increasing responsibilities of the Community, it is no bad thing that the politicians and policy-makers involved should look again at how collective decisions are legitimized at the different levels of government. Ensuring that these institutions are domestically accountable is universally agreed to be important. But so too is the efficiency with which they can discharge their growing functions, especially with the prospect of additional members. Both efficiency and accountability are necessary in a Community which exists to enhance the material and political welfare of its people.

New parliamentary devices: the options

The European Parliament, by virtue of its position as a Community institution, must have first claim to the task of exercising democratic control over Community law-making. It took a major step forward in the rather complicated 'cooperation procedures' which were included in the SEA. But it still remains a long way from being a legislative body. In its report for the IGC prepared by David Martin, a British Labour MEP, it calls for the Parliament and the Council to be given equal rights and equal weight in the legislative process and, as a way to strengthen Parliament's control over the Commission, the right to initiate legislation and to appoint the President of the Commission (on a proposal from the European Council).[5] These recommendations are likely to be resisted by the British and French governments, although they will have the backing of Belgium, Germany and Italy and have gained a substantial measure of support from the Labour Party in Britain. Some enhancement of the Parliament's role will clearly emerge from the IGC.

The ability of the European Parliament properly to reflect the wishes of the people is limited by the different election procedures used in the different member states. Britain is alone in not using a form of proportional representation. There is a strong case for the same system to be used throughout the Community. The European Parliament would also be a more effective body if it were allowed to operate in Brussels only, and did not have to divide its time between Brussels and Strasbourg. There would be widespread sympathy in Britain if this could be achieved, whether through a Treaty amendment or by a *de facto* transfer.

While the responsibilities of the European Parliament should grow, the task of democratic oversight will remain one to be shared with the national parliaments for as long as the Council of Ministers (from the national governments) remains the Community's principal law-maker. This can be done by increasing the national parliaments' involvement with the decision-making process in the Council or by improving their links with the European Parliament, or by a combination of both. While there is room for improving the way the Westminster Parliament handles EC business (and several useful proposals are being implemented or are under consideration), these are matters best left to each national parliament and not prescribed at the Community level. More use can certainly be made of the Select Committee system to allow the British parliament to express its own views and to hold ministers accountable, but there are severe negotiating disadvantages if ministers have to secure too detailed a mandate in advance, as happens in Denmark. A more radical suggestion is that a committee drawn from national parliamentarians should be set up to sit alongside the Council and to express its opinion before decisions are taken. This would be a cumbersome procedure and would be likely to detract from rather than enhance the involvement of national MPs. It would certainly cut across the role of the European Parliament.

The alternative approach is to strengthen the links between the national parliaments and the European Parliament. The case for improved links is strong. In Britain, the Westminster Parliament has treated British MEPs with an absurd degree of condescension and although relations have greatly improved in the last year or so, 'a strong undercurrent of suspicion remains'.[6] Both parties seem anxious to collaborate. Similar concerns are now being expressed in France. Both Michael Heseltine and Giscard d'Estaing have argued in favour of a European Senate or second chamber composed of representatives from the national parliaments. A variant of this proposal, favoured especially in Germany at the Länder level, is that the new chamber should be composed of representatives of the regions rather than of the member states. Either way, creating a third legislative layer would seriously extend an already complicated legislative process. It is doubtful whether it has sufficient advantages over the other improvements discussed here to justify the undoubted loss in terms of efficiency. A more modest suggestion by Bruce Millan, the British Commissioner, is that national parliaments should have some opportunity to meet with the relevant committee in Brussels or Strasbourg before the European Parliament itself

95

debates any proposed piece of EC legislation.[7] This idea could usefully be explored in the dialogue (or 'assizes') which the European Parliament wishes to have with the national parliaments. It would seem better to leave some flexibility by making any such arrangements informal and not enshrined in a treaty.

Effective decision-making: the Council of Ministers

The Council of Ministers is, of all the Community institutions, the body where getting the right balance between democracy and efficiency is most necessary. The Council is where the major decisions are taken. It derives its legitimacy in part from the fact that its members are all ministers responsible to national parliaments; in part through the scrutiny and co-decision processes with the European Parliament; and in part from the consultations with the Economic and Social Committee and other representative bodies. The debate centres on whether these checks are enough. As suggested earlier, there is room for extending the functions of the European Parliament and the diligence of the national parliaments, but not to the extent of making the Council unworkable. Because it is a law-making body, many people would argue that its proceedings should be held in public. While such an idea is superficially attractive, it is certain that the complicated and detailed bargaining process which is essential for a proper compromise would simply be driven underground if the formal Council proceedings were made public.

The tension between accountability and efficiency is well illustrated by the question of majority voting. Some see the issue as an extension of the democratic deficit debate. Decisions taken by majority vote can be considered to be as legitimate as those agreed unanimously in so far as the decisions are taken by duly appointed ministers and the member states have consented to the procedure by ratifying the treaty rules. However, this formal legitimacy might not necessarily guarantee political acceptance within a member state when a government has contested the issue and been outvoted. To be acceptable, majority voting must deal with matters where all the member states have such a common interest in the goals that EC decisions and the prospect of being outvoted are acceptable in national political terms.

The issue now is whether majority voting should be further

extended. There will certainly be strong pressure from some other member states in this direction, as well as from the Commission and the European Parliament. In Britain, the Labour Party now favours extending qualified majority voting to more environmental and social issues. The growing consensus in favour of such a move derives from the awareness that more things get done, or get done more quickly, that way. The Council must be able to act decisively and, if necessary, speedily: to turn rhetoric into substantive decisions. This became evident to the British government during its efforts to impose budgetary restraints and reform the Common Agricultural Policy. It was therefore prepared, when it was clear that achievement of the single market depended on it, to endorse the extension of majority voting in the SEA. Most people in Britain have found this perfectly acceptable, and majority voting has not been politically contentious. Indeed, the House of Commons Select Committee on Foreign Affairs concluded that 'the extension of qualified majority voting which was brought in by the Single European Act has worked to the United Kingdom's advantage'.[8] This verdict, and the success of the 1992 programme, should leave the government free to consider further extension of majority voting in suitable cases. The prospect of further enlargement must greatly strengthen the argument that the Community needs more majority voting if it is to operate effectively.

The Commission: bureaucracy or driving force?

Debate about the European Commission in Britain has seldom risen above the level of cheap jibes at unelected Commissioners and about an inflated and power-hungry bureaucracy. As has been frequently pointed out, the Commission staff (after allowing for the inevitable work of translation and interpretation) is smaller than many Whitehall departments and is now almost certainly *too* small for the tasks which have been assigned to it. The question of the size of the bureaucracy is not, therefore, a serious issue. More serious for Britain has been the under-representation of British nationals at most of the key staffing levels. It is good that the government has introduced new arrangements which should gradually increase the flow of high-quality British personnel into the Commission services. One of the reasons why the French have been so successful in the Community is that they have made sure that the Commission is well staffed with high-calibre French nationals.

As regards the appointment of Commissioners themselves, no serious suggestions have emerged that they should be directly elected or even that they should be drawn from among the members of the European Parliament.[9] Governments seem content to keep the power of appointment in their own hands. This comfortable assumption should not go unchallenged. Given the extent of their responsibilities, the case for giving Commissioners some democratic legitimacy is strong. What better way than to appoint them from among the duly elected members of the European Parliament? To do so would undoubtedly increase the attractiveness of serving as an MEP and thus raise the calibre of the Parliament. In order to retain more of the present balance of powers, the choice of the actual Commissioners could rest, as now, with the member governments, but it would be perfectly possible to envisage them being chosen in due course by the Parliament itself.

Once appointed, Commissioners could either remain MEPs (as in the British system) or (as in other EC countries) resign their seats for as long as they were serving in the Commission. Until such time as the Commissioners are appointed by the European Parliament itself, it seems reasonable that the Parliament should have more say in their appointment or dismissal. This would help to increase the sense of public accountability, although by strengthening the existing alliance between the Commission and the Parliament at the expense of the Council of Ministers, it might not produce the result desired by the critics of unelected Commissioners. To allow the Parliament to sack individual Commissioners (rather than the whole Commission – an option which is open to them at present) would risk undermining the collegiate nature of the Commission.

A different suggestion has been that the Commission of 17 is too big to operate efficiently and that each country should have only one Commissioner. Again, the effect of this suggestion would be to enhance the role of the Commission and diminish the influence of the larger member states. It seems quixotic that such a proposal should have found favour with the present British government. A much better solution would be to have a smaller Commission than the number of member states and to give its members a fixed (non-renewable) term of appointment. That would deal with the problem of having more Commissioners than jobs. It would force the member states to appoint Commissioners who were widely acceptable and perhaps help to reduce the amount of national bargaining which goes on inside the Commission. And it might encourage the appointment of Commissioners of stature and ability. It does not seem a particularly good idea to give a greater role to the President in the choice of other Commissioners since this would only strengthen his position at the expense of the collegiate principle.

It is certainly true that the influence of the Commission has increased with the enlargement of the Community, the growing range and depth of the Community's workload and the enhanced standing of the Community in world affairs. Its formal powers, on the other hand, have remained largely unchanged. It proposes legislation and implements it; but except in defined areas it does not take decisions. Where it does have powers of decision, these are either in the area of management (as with much of the day-to-day running of the CAP) or in areas like competition policy, where it is common to make use of independent agencies.[10] Indeed, it would help to spread the load of responsibility now falling on the Commission and increase transparency if more use were made of agencies like the new European Environmental Agency. The control of European mergers could very well be delegated to an agency at least for the initial evaluation of the competition arguments.[11] The Commission's exclusive right to initiate legislation does give it considerable influence on the course Community business takes, and leverage in the Council negotiations. This leverage has proved to be useful to the Commission in yet another of its roles – helping the Council to find compromise solutions.

The Commission's further duty to act as the first line of defence in securing conformity with Community law is also important. The problems of implementation and compliance have been discussed in Chapter 5 and will clearly be addressed in the IGC. In carrying out its functions, the Commission could with advantage make more use of national enforcement authorities. But, conversely, national governments will probably have to be ready to allow the Commission greater powers of enforcement if rigorous standards are to be secured throughout the Community.

In the exercise of all its functions, the Commission has a large network of formal and informal consultations. Only in the case of the Economic and Social Committee does this network have statutory backing, but in practice it constitutes a very important layer of public accountability, and one which interested groups neglect at their peril. Although much of the Commission's work affects the individual only via the member states, there are nevertheless areas where its actions and decisions do have a direct impact. To safeguard the individual from administrative abuse by Commission officials, the Scandinavian ombudsman system (adopted by several EC countries, including Britain) could be introduced, with appropriate powers and functions. The role of the European Parliament would be enhanced if, as in the British system, a complainant had to approach the ombudsman through an MEP.

Financial accountability

Britain has been successful in getting the whole Community to recognize that, irrespective of the broader issues, there is much to be done in improving financial control of and accountability for Community expenditure. The British experience with the influential Public Accounts Committee of the House of Commons could with advantage be transplanted (with suitable adaptations) into the framework of the European Parliament. In this way the European Parliament, which has in the past had the reputation of being something of a spendthrift, could also acquire the reputation for being an effective watchdog over Community spending.

The European Court of Auditors (itself only set up in 1977, with British encouragement) could be made more effective and give greater assistance to the European Parliament in its watchdog function. The current powers of the Court appear to be unduly restrictive. The forthcoming IGC would be a good opportunity to extend the Court's audit coverage so that it can provide the Council and the Parliament with reasonable assurance as to the accuracy of the accounts prepared by the Commission and the proper regulation of the transactions which underlie them. The work of the Court in scrutinizing financial management and in preparing special reports, e.g. about fraud in the CAP, could be accorded greater status. Finally, since there is now a growing element of Community expenditure which is managed at national level, consideration should be given to ways of improving coordination between the European Court of Auditors and the national audit bodies.

One of the reasons why the European Parliament has a reputation for always pushing the Council to spend more money is the fact that, whereas it has acquired significant powers over the Community budget (i.e. the level and type of expenditure), it has never had any responsibilities for financing it. The Community raises its 'own resources' only to the extent needed to finance the budget and it has therefore not been thought necessary, or – by some people – desirable, to involve the European Parliament in the traditional parliamentary right to be the sole authority to raise taxes. To grant the European Parliament independent powers to raise revenue would be strongly resisted by many member states, not least Britain. Nevertheless, a strong case can be made for giving it *co-responsibility* for the Community's funding, in parallel with its co-responsibility for the budget. This would not mean reducing the Council's powers, since the size of the budget would determine the size of the revenue and the procedures for fixing the budget could remain unchanged. Such a move would be largely symbolic, but it might help to concentrate the minds of European parliamentarians if they were obliged to tell their constituents not only that they had voted for EC assistance for an infrastructure project but that they had voted for an increase in VAT to pay for it!

The principle of subsidiarity

The application of subsidiarity, now one of the EC's key buzz-words though by no means a new concept, is destined to feature prominently in the debate about the future development of the EC.[12] The term is still not well understood in Britain and making it into a practical instrument in the EC will not be easy.[13] It has gained prominence for three reasons: to reassure the doubters that the integration process will not go further than is justified; to ensure that the Community institutions are not overwhelmed with tasks for which they do not have the resources; and to take account of patterns of power-sharing *within* member states.

It is, of course, the first of these which has made the British government so interested in the idea, though the second also echoes British concerns. But what the British government is basically seeking is some explicit recognition that it is the nation-state which carries the highest degree of political legitimacy and that, therefore, it is for the nation-state to decide who does what. That makes subsidiarity an essentially political concept. The Commission, on the other hand, has been approaching the issue from a different angle. It has been endeavouring, over the last two years, to clarify, define and explore just how recourse to a subsidiary test might help to identify the appropriate level of policy authority, using criteria of efficiency, proportionality and judicial soundness. What, for instance, can the subsidiarity principle add to the current debate on EMU? Not an easy question to answer, as the discussion in Chapter 6 has suggested. Perhaps more pertinently, fields such as social and educational policies might, on the analogy of environmental policy, be highlighted as ones where there is scope for real debate and careful judgment about which powers to locate at the EC level and which at the national or regional levels.

During the IGCs, there will be strong pressures to include some words in the Treaties that would define more closely the subsidiarity principle and how it might be applied. There has been support for the idea that it should be incorporated into a substantive article or articles and thus become clearly justiciable, as was argued by the House of Commons Foreign Affairs Committee.[14] In theory such a provision would provide strong constitutional protection against inroads into national sovereignty, with some scope for its enforcement, whether by the European Court or by a special body created for the purpose. Valéry Giscard d'Estaing, for instance, proposed in the European Parliament the creation of an EC equivalent of the French *Conseil constitutionnel*, an institution of the French Fifth Republic enabling a group of prestigious individuals to play a role in maintaining the balance between the public authorities in France.

At the moment, major extensions of Community competence require Treaty amendment and thus offer the complete protection of national ratification by every member state. The real difficulties lie in areas where competencies are concurrent, i.e. shared between the EC and the member states. A subsidiarity clause which through a series of Court rulings increasingly favoured Community action might in the end offer less protection to the national authority than if it had never existed. Indeed, one of the points stressed in the Belgian Memorandum on Institutional Relaunch (see Chapter 10) was the 'evolutionary nature' of the subsidiarity principle. On the other hand, if such a clause were included it could perhaps justify some limitation on those existing Treaty provisions (especially Articles 100 and 235) which have been used, and some would say abused, to carry the Community into new territory.

A further complication is the strong desire of the German Länder to use subsidiarity criteria to prevent the erosion of their powers at the regional level. Regional authorities in other member states might welcome the chance to exploit such an opening, but it seems very unlikely that the member states will be ready to see this issue dealt with at Community level. Whatever the form of any treaty reference to subsidiarity, the criteria for its application will be difficult to define unambiguously. Subsidiarity cannot easily be defined in isolation. Solidarity is often cited as a suitable corollary in the EC context, but it is imprecise. Sovereignty might be offered as a counterweight, but it too defies clear definition. Efficiency is emerging in the current debate as a favoured runner. While subsidiarity will be needed to strike a political balance at the IGC which is acceptable to Britain, entrenching it would be no panacea.

A plan for Britain

What, then, should be Britain's contribution to this continuing debate on institutional reform? Fortunately there are signs that, even though some will prefer to speak of an IGC on 'political union', the reality looks like being more correctly labelled 'institutional reform'. This will chime in better with the British preference for dealing with these questions gradually and cautiously, as befits a country with no written constitution or bill of rights of its own.

The Foreign Secretary, Douglas Hurd, has suggested four guiding ideas: to make the Community more democratic and closer to the citizen; to make the Community institutions work better; to accord respect for the subsidiarity principle; and to ensure that the Community remains liberal and open to the world.[15] These are realizable aims and would be consistent with proposing:

(i) *In the interests of greater efficiency*

(a) extension of majority voting into additional areas by analogy with the success of the Single European Act;

(b) a Commission of, say, nine, appointed from the European Parliament by the member states, endorsed by the European Parliament, and with a six-year non-renewable term;

(c) provision for setting up agencies, by analogy with the European Environmental Agency, with a degree of independence from the Commission in areas such as competition policy; and

(d) provisions, including financial penalties, for non-compliance with the rulings of the European Court and greater enforcement powers for a Commission cooperating with national authorities;

(ii) *In the interests of greater accountability*

(a) more effective scrutiny by national parliaments;
(b) strengthened links between the national parliaments and MEPs, but on an informal basis;
(c) extension of the cooperation procedure with the European Parliament to all decisions of the Council taken by majority vote;
(d) endorsement of the principle of subsidiarity;
(e) strengthening the powers of the European Court of Auditors and the responsibilities of the European Parliament for effective financial control of expenditure; and
(f) appointment of a Community ombudsman by analogy with British practice.

Proposals of this kind could yield valuable gains for the quality of Community decision-making in the short to medium term. All of them build on the existing infrastructure and work with rather than against the grain of the current division of powers between the Community institutions and the member states. They also recognize that in those cases where the EC acts as the vehicle of collective decisions and shared legislation, its institutions must be empowered to do a proper job.

Any remaining doubt about these proposals has to be not about whether they adequately respond to the real or perceived democratic deficit, but about whether they would sufficiently improve the Community's effectiveness to enable it to cope with an extended membership. The IGC will need to keep this prospect well to the fore if the dual aim of 'deepening' and 'widening' is to be achieved. If it adopts such an approach, and as heady rhetoric on political union gives way to more cautious progress based upon adaptation of existing structures, Britain can find itself close to the centre ground of the debate – or even, should it espouse the proposals set out here for the Commission, taking the lead.

10

THE COMMUNITY'S GOALS

'I will set this foot of mine as far
'As who goes farthest'
– JULIUS CAESAR

Britain's aspirations

Britain has a reputation for pragmatism. With that goes a dislike for the grand design or for speculation about what the French call *finalités* – in other words, ultimate goals. This is very evident in the current debate about political union and where the EC is heading. Among the British political parties, only the Liberal Democrats have been ready to use federal language and to welcome the prospect of a federal Europe, with appropriate levels of power defined for the Community, the member states and the regions. The Labour Party rejects a United States of Europe in favour of 'closer and closer' cooperation, but has not yet been at all specific about how far this might go. The position of the Social Democrats was not dissimilar. The Green Party has a strong internationalist perspective, but has been highly critical of the EC for its emphasis on growth strategies and market forces as crucial to environmental conservation. Interestingly, the Scottish National Party has now espoused the cause of European integration, in the belief that it could provide a framework for a viable independent Scotland.

The Conservative manifesto for the 1989 European elections called for 'a Europe of independent states cooperating freely in a climate of economic liberty'. However, as was argued in Chapter 2, that was little more than an attempt to paper over the cracks which

105

had emerged within the party. Surrounding the bulk of moderate pro-Europeans are the enthusiasts on one wing, who would be prepared to go as far and as fast as the rest of the Community, and, on the other, the Bruges Group hardliners who accept and welcome the single market, but reject further transfers of political power. For these last, the *finalité* of Europe has already been reached.

Given this diversity of views, it is small wonder that the British public remains confused, though apparently less inhibited about integration than the present British government. It seems likely that the hesitations and uncertainties would diminish if there were a strong and consistent political lead. Perhaps more than other member states, the British are inclined to look at the Community exclusively through their own, often parochial, telescope and to be insufficiently aware of views elsewhere in the Community, which need to be taken into account. The remainder of this chapter therefore looks at the aims and insights of Britain's partners.[1]

Germany

German perspectives are particularly important. Not only does the German economy carry great weight in the EC, but the Federal Republic has been one of the leading advocates of a politically united Europe. Unification will not change that attitude, though the fears that unification brought on made German politicians acutely aware of the need to express a permanent commitment to the integration of the Community and a wider Europe. But it goes deeper than that. There is recognition that 'we Germans certainly owe a decisive share of our country's democratic strength – not to mention our prosperity – to our membership of a community of free nations'.[2] For the Federal Republic, the evolution towards closer European integration has been a natural, step-by-step progression, enhanced by the growth of trust among the member states in shared Community objectives. Germans have accepted the pooling of sovereignty which has resulted from this process, perhaps more easily than most because of their federal system.

The target of completing the single market, which enjoys a widespread consensus in the Bundestag, sets much of the integrative pace, although the conditions of stability which had helped the embedding of integration have been altered by the recent events in the rest of Europe. The Community, according to German consensus, is now under challenge to define some new targets, in the sense that political integration is a means for the EC to consolidate its achievements and thus respond positively to the dramatic changes in Europe. There is broad acceptance in Germany that the fields of economic, security and environmental policy also need to be drawn into the integration process. Equally, most Germans accept the principle of EMU; but nervousness that a European system might put at risk Germany's postwar success in laying the ghost of inflation, and understandable preoccupations with implementing Germany's own monetary union (the GEMU), have both led to some divided counsels.

Enlargement of the EC, which many Germans see as inevitable, will result in pressures to make EC decision-making more efficient and democratic. The German government has favoured a streamlining of decision-making mechanisms and has been an outspoken supporter of stronger powers for the European Parliament. Such an institutional reform would ideally prompt closer links between the European Parliament and legislatures in the member states – for the Germans this means regional as well as national bodies. As a result of its own federal experience, the German government favours a clarification of the division of power between the EC and the member states. While this recital might suggest that Germany comes into the 'maximalist' category among European integrationists, it does have other preoccupations which may make its performance more moderate than the rhetoric.

France

President Mitterrand declared after the Dublin European Council of June 1990 that political union in Europe should have a *finalité fédérale*. His recurrent use of federalist language marks an important shift in the French political debate about the EC. In the past, and particularly during the period of high Gaullism, the French were the nationalists of Europe – reluctant to let integrationist moves in the EC penetrate too far into the powers of the French state. Their negotiators concentrated on moving specific EC policies in a direction congruent with French policies.

However, this profile has changed radically over the past decade and has produced a consensus across the core of the political spectrum (though not always on the outer fringes) on two issues:

first, that the French have no option other than a strong commitment to the integration process itself; and, second, that their old worries about the erosion of national sovereignty were misplaced. The important point for the current French government and any likely successor government is to concentrate on influencing the EC debate on all issues as effectively as possible. It was this realization, reinforced by their difficult experiences in the early 1980s, that led French policy-makers and entrepreneurs to conclude that the internal market programme was both necessary and desirable for the French economy. The EMS did the same job for French monetary policy, which explains the French enthusiasm for EMU.

Such judgments have redoubled weight in the French debate now that German unification has been so rapidly implemented. Of course, there are worries in France about the economic and political consequences of Germany, its key neighbour, becoming larger and more confident. But the political inference has been unambiguous: the EC must be strengthened and the French government must work closely with its German counterpart to maintain a constructive partnership.[3]

What does all of this mean in practice? First, French politicians have become much more sympathetic to proposals for institutional reform, as is reflected in the often heady rhetoric about political union. This sympathy is, however, matched by considerable prudence on specifics, where French negotiators are likely to endorse gradual rather than radical alterations in the Treaty rules. Second, the French government is using the window of opportunity provided by the internal market programme to change the thrust of previous French policy and practice. The transition is difficult and not without points of resistance, but the commitment seems well embedded. Third, French positions on EC issues have become much less monolithic, reflecting differences in political and policy perspectives. One indication of this is the very active part played by several prominent French politicians in the European Parliament.

Italy

Italian decision-makers since the 1950s have always considered EC membership beneficial to the domestic political and economic system, and in this they have had full public support. In their view, European culture and values are to be shared, and the pooling of sovereignty in the EC presents no problem. During its Presidency of the Community (July-December 1990), Italy has shown enthusiasm for the two IGCs, but interestingly has been much less maximalist than at the time of the SEA. Italians argue that all EC institutions need reinforcement of powers, not least because this could also bring benefit to their own tumultuous domestic political system. It would be useful for them if the European Parliament were to enjoy full powers of decision-making, along with the Council of Ministers, and a greater role in controlling the implementation and observance of EC legislation. Italian membership of the EMS has probably helped the national economy; EMU would be a new challenge, and a difficult one for Italy to meet, but there would be no doubting its political commitment. However, it is not a foregone conclusion that Italy could be a full participant in EMU straight away.

Italian ideas on the Community's external policies are also of increasing relevance. As earlier chapters have shown, the Italians have strong views about the EC's role and policies in the Mediterranean and the Middle East and, because of their historical connections with their neighbours in southeast Europe, have been developing new relationships as a result of current developments in the region. These factors also make the Italian government look favourably on eventual enlargement, seeing Austria as the first candidate.

Spain

Although a relative newcomer to the Community, the Spanish government has become an explicit supporter of the proposals for economic, monetary and political union and a keen advocate of closer European integration. It maintains excellent contacts with President Delors and the Commission and also with the German and French governments. It sees the forthcoming IGCs as the occasion for a 'qualitative jump forward', providing for full EMU, common European citizenship, and a common foreign and security policy.[4]

Spain understandably puts emphasis on the economic and social cohesion of the Community. The importance of the regional dimension is reflected in the outspoken support for the Community expressed in Catalonia and the Spanish Basque country. Spain supports EMU but wants to see the economic aspect emphasised as much as the monetary one. It has shown interest in British ideas for an indeterminate stage before the EC moves to permanently locked exchange rates. Above all, it does not want to be left behind in a two-speed EMU.

Spain has made the issue of common citizenship in the Community one of its major objectives, wishing to see the Treaty include a definition of citizenship and a list of political, social and economic rights and obligations for all Community citizens. The Spanish government takes a positive view of institutional reform but does not want to see the delicate balance of decision-making disturbed. It recognizes the relevance of subsidiarity, though as a political rather than a legal definition. The underlying message is that Spain wants to see an EC with a 'global and balanced approach' to future development, one that goes beyond the purely economic horizon and that is supplied with adequate financial resources.

Other member states

The *Benelux* countries have provided an important counterweight to the ideas of the larger EC states on future directions of the Community. All three tend to favour rather strong powers for EC institutions, to accept notions of political union and to use federal language. The Dutch favour an emphasis on efficiency as well as democratic controls; they would welcome a slimming down of the Commission to one member per EC state and have recently indicated some support for the idea of a European Senate with equal representation for each member state. They wish to work towards a common defence and foreign policy. Belgium was first in the field, with its proposals for the IGCs. Interestingly, for a country known for its integrationist views, the proposals contained in the Memorandum on Institutional Relaunch of March 1990 do not amount to a blueprint for European union. They are comparatively modest: more powers of co-decision for the Parliament, general use of majority voting, and election of the Commission's President by the Parliament.

The shift in *Danish* policy is interesting. Danish politicians remain reticent about a common foreign policy and a strong European Parliament. But they now acknowledge the compelling need to strengthen EC institutions – a major reversal of their previous, more hesitant, policy. This means that they no longer automatically align themselves with Britain in resisting further transfers of sovereignty, including EMU. The Danish government also welcomes the idea of 'non-exclusive' enlargement: 'The Community pulls the European train and is the dynamo of European development. We must continue to strengthen the integration process within the EEC itself.'[5]

The *Portuguese* take a cautious approach. From their position on the periphery of the EC, they worry about their economic opportunities and the possible consequences of the investment race in Eastern Europe. Further integration or enlargement would not be especially helpful to them.

This is to be contrasted with *Irish* policy, in which peripheral geographic position has been offset by vigorous efforts to match Community policies to Irish needs. Of course, this has been partly impelled by the welcome opportunity to distinguish Irish from British policy, best symbolized by the participation of the Irish punt in the EMS and the associated rupture of monetary union with the UK. On broader EC issues, Irish policy remains close to the Community centre ground.

The story of *Greek* policy within the EC has been less happy. The deep problems of Greek politics and the economy have led to an introversion by policy-makers and a consequential lack of influence in EC developments. The new government is seeking to retrieve this but has a lot of ground to recover.

The other West Europeans

The IGC on institutional reform has come at an awkward time in the negotiations between the EC and EFTA. As discussed in Chapter 3, the concept of a European Economic Area found favour as a means of squaring the circle of achieving an internal market covering the wider Western Europe, associating EFTA with relevant decision-making and leaving space for the EC of 12 to deepen its own integration politically and economically. But the prospect that the tolerant pragmatism of the EEA might not work, and the events in Eastern Europe, have led to some furious rethinking in EFTA countries. However, just at the point where real debates were opening about accepting the old set of EC aims and practices, the EC appears to be determined to move the goal-posts.

The resulting dilemmas are nowhere felt more keenly than in Switzerland, so detached from the formal process of integration while at the same time so deeply integrated with the EC economically. Swiss policy-makers, politicians and entrepreneurs have swiftly come to acknowledge that they too may have a circle to square. Already Switzerland has applied to join the World Bank and the IMF, and, more remarkable still, joined in the UN sanctions against Iraq. These moves imply a redefinition of neutrality and might produce a different policy on EC membership. At such a point, the Swiss are bound to hope that the EC will not rush too far down the road of political integration. And they might, with some justice, feel that they could contribute to the debate about the shape of the EC, given their very special confederal structure. From this springs a conviction that collaboration can be combined with differentiation – ideas which will appeal to some but not all member states. They can certainly offer experience in applying the subsidiarity principle: 'Subsidiarity has been an appropriate guideline between the Swiss cantons and the Confederation and it can perhaps be valuable too in a European context.'[6]

A summing-up

It is possible to draw a number of tentative conclusions from this survey of other European views. First, in most EC member states there is widespread acceptance that further integration should be encouraged, though naturally a range of views about what that should imply. Each country has its own rhetoric and its own political agenda but all of them are pointing in the same direction as regards the future of the EC.

Second, the growth in the political and economic weight of the Community over the past years makes it increasingly difficult to separate its political ambitions from its economic ones. Support for EMU and political union tend to go together.

Third, while there is widespread recognition that the new European political configuration provides a great window of opportunity which should not be allowed to close, no one is very clear about the long-term implications for the EC. Support for further enlargement of the Community is distinctly muted, with the most enthusiastic integrationists and the poorer member states being the most reticent.

Fourth, it is not possible to rely on nationality as the key determinant of preferences, since ideological and party views are often more relevant. Thus the views of the government of the day may reflect only one national viewpoint, and may change with changing political fortunes. What will happen in the Community will be influenced by the prevailing political mood of the times.[7]

Lastly, what seems to be emerging at present is a preference for the integration process in Europe to move forward, but to do so flexibly and even rather pragmatically. If a European federation is the goal, it is not for today or tomorrow. A 'super-state' is wanted by nobody. But there is a widely shared determination that the EC *should* move forward, that it be effective and that its decisions rest on a bedrock of legitimacy.

11

AN AGENDA FOR BRITAIN

'On such a full sea we are now afloat
'And we must take the current when it serves
'Or lose our ventures'
– JULIUS CEASAR

Britain's destiny lies with the European Community. This is now recognized by the majority of the British people, by an overwhelming proportion of the country's wealth creators and by the leadership of all the major parties. It was perhaps inevitable that Britain took a long time to come to this position, and we have paid a price for it. But that is now behind us, and the penalties that we now incur are of our own making. As a result of the many changes taking place in Europe, new issues have been raised and new opportunities presented, in response to which the voice of Britain will be welcomed by its European partners.

Britain can respond to the current German readiness to be locked into a European community; nothing could be better for the future peace and safety of Europe.[1] There is no reason to doubt that this can be achieved. But the only available route to it is via an EC within which the member states are more closely bound together. France has perceived this, but British support will greatly increase the chance of it happening. More British nationalism can only breed more German nationalism.

Britain can respond to the growing importance of the EC in world affairs. During the postwar period, Britain made a great contribution to the security of Europe in the building up of NATO and the American commitment to European defence. But it stood aside from

114

the economic integration process. Now there are new challenges in Europe; there has been a shifting throughout the world of the power-base that had existed since the end of the Second World War; and economics, politics and defence are much more intertwined than they were. Britain is no longer a world power. Its contribution to this complex of economic, financial and strategic challenges has to come through the EC. It has diplomatic skills, imagination and experience to bring. These will best be deployed as part of the European team.

As the preceding chapter has shown, the prevailing mood among the other Community countries is one of determination to press on towards closer economic and political integration without necessarily being clear what the final stage might look like. None of them has in mind a single European government or the disappearance of the nation-state. In the process of moving closer together, step by step, it remains a journey to an unknown destination.[2] There is unanimity about the direction but diversity about pace and mode and the likely end-point.

Britain, like any other member state, has every right to its own views on these important questions. We can exercise choice about where we put the weight of our effort within the Community, but it is a choice which has to take account of the views of our partners. We can be as confident as we like about the rightness of our cause, but unless we can carry others in the Community with us it will get us nowhere. Thus any attempt to re-create a Gaullist view of Europe[3] – based simply on cooperation between independent sovereign states – is doomed to failure. The French themselves no longer believe that that is sufficient and it has no support among the other member states. The reality of the EC integration process has already gone far beyond such a concept – with the agreement of successive British governments and the endorsement of the British parliament – and there is no turning back. The range of choice for Britain has to be within the boundaries of the possible, and our ability to influence the course of events will depend on positioning ourselves within those boundaries.

What we can do is to choose whether we wish to try to slow the process down and run the risk, if necessary, of being part of a slower group in a two-speed Europe, or whether we wish to put our energies into ensuring that the process develops as nearly as possible in the way we would like. Or put another way: 'Should a British government consider it vital to play an active role in shaping the future direction of European cooperation; or should it do its best to retain a degree of autonomy and capacity for independent action, leaving its Continental neighbours the initiative in defining the rules of European cooperation?"[4] Put either way, the choice seems obvious. Given the premise, it seems difficult to formulate the question in a neutral manner. Of course, the fact of the matter is that in reality we can do a bit of both. No one will expect the British suddenly to become the most ardent federalists in Europe. Nor should we stop negotiating hard for British commercial or other interests. That too would be out of character, foolish and unnecessary. But we could make a policy shift, as the Danes have done, from being dragged along kicking and screaming in the wake of the majority to a recognition that the national interest may best be served by working with the grain and playing the game the Community way.

Tactics in the Community

Britain's membership of the EC now extends over almost 20 years, and experience suggests that our position would be more comfortable and our influence enhanced if we learned some lessons from our own mistakes and the successes of our partners. The most important would seem these:

(a) *Build alliances*. This is already the meat and drink of day-to-day negotiations in Brussels but, as argued in Chapter 4, we need to get closer to our Community partners, especially France and Germany, and be ready to compromise in order to set up a winning hand. And we need to understand that the attitude to political rhetoric in other countries is not the same as ours, and that it gives offence if we sneer or imply a lack of sincerity.

(b) *Avoid the 'them' and 'us' attitude*. The EC requires continuous negotiation, in which British interests have to be fought for, but it fosters public antagonism towards the Community if every Council meeting is portrayed as a battleground. Every deal is by definition a triumph, but let it be a triumph for the Community (of which we are part).

(c) *Take initiatives*. Britain has often been criticized for not being sufficiently pro-active. It is certainly true that it pays to get in early with an idea so as to sell it, if possible, to the Commission.[5] But when our positions are so extreme as to be outside the achievable, it inhibits initiatives. The more we can position ourselves within the debate, the more pro-active we can and should be. The French act as though (and sometimes make people believe) what is good for France is good for the Community. We could do the same.

(d) *Use the 'yes, but ...' approach.* Experience in the Community suggests that a satisfactory result can often be achieved more readily, not by attacking a proposal from the outset, but by seeking to make it acceptable by subsequent amendment. With our reputation for instant opposition, this is an approach which could be tried with benefit.[6]

(e) *Make the most of Britain's considerable influence in the Community.* This final point may appear obvious, but in view of earlier strictures it is important to stress that we *are* important members of the Community and have the ability to achieve results. The present British government has wanted, as every government tends to do, to shape the Community in its own image, and in recent years it has had considerable success in doing so, notably in pushing forward the completion of the single market and in introducing budgetary discipline into the Common Agricultural Policy.[7] Among the business communities of the EC, Britain is seen as an active and enthusiastic partner, and one to be respected. Moreover, we play a leading part in the work of foreign policy cooperation (EPC). No one doubts our negotiating skills. On some occasions, when it suits our partners to accuse us of being bad Europeans (as it did during the budget controversies), that may be more than anything else a tribute to our effectiveness.

Improvements at home

On the domestic scene, three issues are of importance for Britain's place in the Community. They are interconnected. The first is the prospect of greater political consensus over Europe; the second concerns the improvement in public understanding of the EC; and the third relates to the sovereignty question.

With the shift in Labour Party policy, there is for the first time some prospect in Britain of moving towards a cross-party agreement on some of the broader issues of European integration. This could be of considerable value to Britain's standing in the Community. Both France and Germany have influence in the EC not only because of their size, position and wealth, but because their policies towards the Community enjoy wide political support in their own countries. The same could be true in Britain. We can expect specific EC policy issues to be argued over between the parties in the usual way, but in negotiation on the more general issues our views will carry greater weight if it is known that they carry broad political backing and do not risk being overturned at the next general election.

In spite of having arguably the best serious media coverage of the EC of any country, the level of understanding and interest in Britain is disappointingly low. People are confused by the conflicting signals coming from different ministers and by the apparent gap between what ministers say and what they actually agree to in Brussels. But the lack of understanding must be attributed largely to the unwillingness of successive governments to present the EC to the public in a favourable light. They have not wished by so doing to undermine their negotiating position in Brussels; nor have they cared to take the risk of being accused by the Opposition of propaganda.

With the possibility of cross-party agreement, and the end of the great battles between Britain and the rest of the Community over the budget, these objections now have little validity. The government's 1992 campaign was successful in raising the level of business awareness of the opportunities and challenges of the single market. What is now required is a more low-key, but wider and more sustained, effort to raise understanding about the impact on the citizen, about attitudes elsewhere in the Community, about the real nature of sovereignty, about other forms of democracy in Europe, about the nature of the EC process, about the role of the European Parliament, about American attitudes towards the EC and Britain's place in it, about what subsidiarity means – the list is a long one. This is not a plea for propaganda but for increased understanding of what the EC is about. If a national programme could form part of an EC-wide effort to explain the relevance of the Community, so much the better.

The public is particularly confused over the sovereignty issue. The extent to which powers have already been transferred to the EC is often not fully recognized. Nor is the extent to which the *de facto* sovereignty of the economic and financial market has made the question of *de jure* sovereignty an academic one. The question of further transfers is bedevilled by the quite separate question of whether the EC process is necessarily more bureaucratic than the national one. And, as discussed in Chapter 2, the peculiarities of the British system have given the Westminster parliament a vested interest in the status quo. Some important constitutional issues are already coming under increasing scrutiny in Britain. It is important that the debate should be conducted in a way which squarely faces the realities of the sovereignty issue and which takes full account of Britain's membership of the EC, the fact that that membership is likely to grow in importance as we move towards the twenty-first century, and the likely way in which the Community itself will evolve. Are there changes in our procedures or in Community procedures which would reduce the gap between British and Continental perceptions of political accountability? What should be the long-run division of responsibility between the Westminster and the European parliaments? What would be the implications of having different electoral systems for the two bodies? It might be hoped that, given their relatively more detached position, their legal expertise and their accumulated and widely admired expertise in EC and constitutional matters, the European Communities Committee of the House of Lords would at least start this process off.

Issues for the EC

The questions facing the Community itself over the next few years really boil down to two: how much more should the member states do together, and should other countries be allowed to join in? The first of these questions encompasses most of the topics discussed in this study. From Britain's point of view it is obviously helpful that the concept of subsidiarity should now be so widely accepted as a valid element in the choice. In spite of all the ambiguities discussed in Chapter 9, there should nevertheless be reassurance for those who fear the centripetal effect of the Community. But the principle needs to be applied with objectivity and not as a blind reflex to resist the transfer of responsibility from the national to the Community level when this would be likely to make more sense or bring benefit. And once the decision to make the switch has been taken, then we should avoid fighting an institutional rearguard action to try to maintain the veneer of national control.

The first big test will come with the two IGCs, when Britain's performance will be watched with great care by its partners. This study has made suggestions for a constructive British approach to institutional reform and how we might handle what may prove to be the more difficult question of EMU. The fact that the two conferences are being held side by side is no accident. It reflects the recognition that, as the EC moves towards economic and monetary union, the strengthening of its democratic structures becomes essential. It will severely test the capabilities of the system, even with the changes which are proposed (which some will find already too ambitious). The need for an informed debate becomes greater as EMU moves into sensitive political territory. The business world understands and welcomes the direction of EMU and does not fully share the politicians' concern with some of the political consequences. The political world understands the consequences and therefore remains cautious about the move. Each needs to listen to the other. It would be a tragedy if Britain found itself unable to go along with this next major step in the EC's development.

The IGCs, whatever their outcome, are only part of the story. The spill-over effect of the 1992 programme is already carrying the Community into grey areas, such as border controls, and having consequences on domestic policies like social security which are bound to enhance its influence. The Community is taking on new responsibilities which will strain its financial resources and raise the need for a larger Community budget. These are all areas of Community policy in which Britain has traditionally had great difficulties. Other member states will have problems with them too; hence the need for alliances. It will be important that these issues are balanced by others where Britain will have a more positive role. The internal market, nature conservation, external trade policy, financial accountability, the role of the EC in political cooperation and European security are all areas in which – whether in the context of the IGC or not – British initiatives would be welcome to our EC partners and desirable in themselves.

Unless we can show our commitment to the continued internal development and strengthening of the EC in these ways, British views on the Community's external relations will be discounted. Yet it is precisely here that Britain has probably the most influential and necessary contribution to make. The EC must remain an open trading partner, in its own interests as much as for the sake of the open-market system. It needs to be generous in its treatment of its close Mediterranean neighbours, its traditional ties with the ACP, and now – through Spain and Portugal – with Latin America. It needs to find an accommodation with the EFTA countries. It needs to play a full part in the CSCE process and be open to new arrangements as the new security situation in Europe unfolds. And it needs to be open to Eastern Europe, assisting the process of building stable democracies and making it clear that, as such, they will be welcome as potential members of an enlarged Community. The EC has shied away before from increasing its size for fear of compromising its cohesion. Each time that it has successfully absorbed new members it has shown that widening and deepening can both be achieved. The next time may be more difficult but it need not be impossible. It would be a worthy objective for the Community for the next few years. It is one to which, provided we subscribe equally to both the deepening and the widening, Britain could make a notable contribution.

Europe – the future

In 1984, Mrs Thatcher presented her fellow heads of government in the European Council with a paper entitled 'Europe – the Future'.[8] It got little publicity within Britain, but it was well received by the other EC governments and helped to carry the Community forward in the way many British wanted. A lot of its message holds good today.[9] But circumstances have greatly changed in the intervening years. We might now offer the Community a new set of objectives for the early 1990s along the following lines:

(a) *to reap the full economic benefits of a single market.* This will require pressure to complete the 1992 programme in full; further measures to achieve liberalization, especially in transport; improvement in the terms of measures already decided, especially in financial services; and full implementation and compliance throughout the EC.

(b) *to promote economic and monetary convergence as rapidly as possible.* This will require early agreement to the next stages of EMU so that the aim of a single currency within the next decade becomes realistic. It will mean readiness to consider aids to economic convergence, including the use of a redistributive EC budget.

(c) *to make the Community more accountable to its citizens,* politically and financially. This must happen in parallel with the extension of Community powers in EMU and other areas. It will

121

require giving greater powers of co-decision and greater responsibility for tax-raising and control of expenditure to the European Parliament, and using both national and European parliaments to scrutinize more closely the work of the Council and the Commission.

(d) *to make the Community more accessible to its citizens.* This will require progress in those activities such as environmental protection, education, ease of travel and conditions of work which touch people directly. It will involve the EC as a whole (reinforcing national information programmes) in developing common themes which will present the Community in a more favourable light.

(e) *to make the Community more efficient.* This will require more majority voting, swifter enforcement, a greater use of agencies and a compact Commission. Proposals are made in Chapter 9.

(f) *to strengthen democracy and reinforce political stability throughout Europe.* This will require sustained technical and financial support for the newly democratic countries of Eastern Europe and an expressed willingness to welcome them as members of the EC on a phased basis, as proposed in Chapter 3. It will also involve the EC playing a constructive role in the CSCE process and assisting the Soviet Union through its political and economic transformation.

(g) *to support the open trading system.* This will call for fresh ideas to deal with world trade and debt problems, closer monetary cooperation and a clamp-down on protectionist pressures. It will mean an appropriate follow-up to the GATT Uruguay Round, improved trading relations with Japan and the United States, and further moves towards a more market-oriented CAP.

(h) *to enhance the standing and effectiveness of the EC as an influence in world affairs.* This will require a programme for the progressive introduction of a common foreign policy and the integration of the EC and EPC processes, on lines discussed in Chapter 4.

(j) *to contribute to the security of Europe in the light of the changing threats.* This will mean developing new security systems in cooperation with NATO allies and possibly taking on the role of WEU. It will need a more open market for defence procurement and closer defence collaboration between EC countries.

(k) *to play a responsible role in encouraging the progress of developing countries.* This will require not only aid but the opening of the

EC market, especially in favour of the rapidly growing countries of North Africa and those with special links with the Community through the ACP agreements.

After the events of 1989, no one can predict with any confidence how the EC will in practice develop during the coming years. Its own history is one of alternating periods of vigour and stagnation. It is possible that it will find itself in another trough of immobility, though at present that looks unlikely. It may well have to contend with periods of strong internal conflict. The strains of German unification may prove greater than the early successes would suggest. An economic recession could put back the single market process or create intolerable social or economic adjustment problems for certain regions. Economic divergences could lead to the collapse of EMU. The Community could find itself at loggerheads over the issue of enlargement and its relationships with the countries of Eastern Europe. The external uncertainties must be even greater. There could be a serious split with the US over trade or defence policy. Serious instability outside the EC, whether in the Soviet Union, Eastern Europe or the Middle East, could create friction among the member states as to what the EC's collective response should be. On the other hand, a serious new threat to Western Europe might act as a powerful unifying force. A break-up of the Soviet Union would present the Community with a different set of challenges.

With so many areas of uncertainty, it is in Britain's interest – just as much as in that of any other member state – for the Community to be robust, and capable of reacting quickly, effectively and, above all, flexibly. The uncertainty is, in itself, an argument for greater cohesion. Alongside these great events, the EC will continue to deal with the myriad small but important issues which make up the life of its institutions. As Christopher Tugendhat has written, the EC is like a cathedral, a combination of grand architecture and the minutiae of everyday life.[10] Britain is inextricably part of this complex, but with a reputation for being more at home with the latter than with the former. The prospects are exciting, to be welcomed more than to be feared. By all means let Britain act in the future more as though what is good for Britain is good for the Community; but we need also to believe that what is good for the Community may be good for Britain.

NOTES

Chapter 2

1 An opinion poll commissioned by the EC Commission and quoted by Uwe Kitzinger in *Diplomacy and Persuasion: How Britain Joined the Common Market* (Thames and Hudson, London, 1973) showed that in 1970 only 18% of the British sample wanted to join the EC, whereas enthusiasm elsewhere in the Community was great – ranging from 51% in Italy to 79% in the Netherlands, where the strong support for British membership at the time has gradually given way to considerable disillusionment. To the question, 'Assuming Britain did join, would you be for or against the evolution of the common market towards the political formation of a United States of Europe?', 75% said 'yes' in Luxembourg, 69% in West Germany, 67% in France, 64% in the Netherlands, 60% in Belgium and Italy, and only 30% in Britain.

2 Reared in the confrontational atmosphere of the House of Commons, British ministers in any case often have difficulty in adjusting to the atmosphere and negotiating style of the EC's Council of Ministers. Many of them do it very successfully. If it does not happen, the result looks to the rest of the Community like xenophobia.

3 In, for example, *Faltering Leviathan: a Report on National Sovereignty, the Regions and Europe*, prepared by David Marquand for the Wyndham Place Trust, London, in 1989. These paragraphs draw heavily on an additional paper which Professor Marquand provided for this study.

4 Ibid.

5 Speech given by the Rt Hon. Margaret Thatcher to the Aspen Institute, Colorado, 5 August 1990.

6 Sir Michael Butler, *Europe: More than a Continent* (Heinemann, London, 1986), p. 169.

7 For an analysis of these contradictions, see William and Helen Wallace, 'Strong State or Weak State in Foreign Policy: the Contradictions of Conservative Liberalism, 1979–87', *Public Administration*, vol. 68 (1990), no. 1.

8 The minority view was articulated, among others, by former Trade and Industry Secretary Nicholas Ridley, whose views on Germany, as expressed in an article in *The Spectator* on 14 July 1990, led to his resignation from the government, but who is just as passionately opposed to further EC integration (see interview in the *Sunday Express*, 10 August 1990).

9 Reported in *Eurobarometer*, no. 31 (EC Commission, Brussels, June 1989), p. A8, Table 2.

10 Published in the *Daily Telegraph*, 12 June 1989.

11 Gallup Report, *Industrialists and City Survey*, London, June 1989.

12 The trade figures in Table 1 relate to visible exports and imports. Britain's invisible trade has been growing faster, but the share of the total taken by the EC has remained stubbornly down, at around 30%. This suggests that there should be scope for significant expansion as the 1992 programme begins to bite in the financial services sector.

Chapter 3

1 Helen Wallace, *Widening and Deepening: The European Community and the New European Agenda*, Discussion Paper 23 (RIIA, London, 1989), p. v.

2 William Wallace, *The Transformation of Western Europe* (RIIA/Pinter, London, 1990), p. 100.

3 J.M.C. Rollo et al., *The New Eastern Europe: Western Responses* (RIIA/Pinter, London, 1990), p. 133.

4 Article 237 of the Treaty of Rome says that 'any European country may apply to become a member of the Community'.

5 If Turkey joined the EC, it would be easily the largest member state by 2010.

6 See Helen Wallace, *Widening and Deepening*.

7 Ibid., p. 28.

8 See, for example, Christopher Tugendhat, *Making Sense of Europe* (Viking, London, 1986), for discussion of the concept of 'concentric circles'. Also the article 'A vision of Europe' by Michael Mertes and Norbert Prill, which occasioned some interest when it appeared in the

Frankfurter Allgemeine Zeitung on 19 July 1989 because, at the time, both authors were working in the office of the Federal Chancellor in Bonn. While it was doubtless a piece of kite-flying, it is not clear how far the German government subscribes to these ideas. Its experience in dealing with the problems of East Germany will no doubt influence its attitude to possible EC membership for East European countries.

Chapter 4

1 *The Financial Times*, 12 June 1990.
2 Extract from the declaration of the NATO summit meeting, London, 6 July 1990.
3 William Wallace, *The Transformation of Western Europe* (RIIA/Pinter, London, 1990).
4 See Robert Marjolin, *Memoirs 1911–1986* (Weidenfeld and Nicolson, London, 1989), for a good insight into the crucial role played by the US in fostering the early postwar movement towards European integration.
5 Sir Derek Thomas, former British Political Director, whose paper on the development and future development of EPC formed the basis for this section of the study, though he is not committed to the conclusions.
6 Paper prepared for this study by David Nicholls, former Deputy Secretary, Ministry of Defence.
7 Declaration of the NATO summit meeting, London, 6 July 1990. Italics added.
8 Speech by Sir Leon Brittan, Vice-President of the EC Commission, to the British Atlantic Group of Young Politicians, London, 17 May 1990.
9 Interview with *Le Figaro* reported in *The Financial Times*, 7 July 1990.
10 For a fascinating analysis of Anglo-French relations, see Françoise de La Serre, Jacques Leruez and Helen Wallace, (eds.), *French and British Foreign Policies in Transition: The Challenge of Adjustment* (RIIA/ CERI/Berg, London, Paris and Oxford, 1990).
11 Writing in *The Independent*, 2 August 1990, Dominique Moisi, Associate Director of the Institut Français des Relations Internationales, says: 'Britain has to abandon its dream of perpetuating its special relationship with the US, and engage itself fully in the European adventure. It cannot leave France and Germany to stare at each other when the meaning and boundaries of Europe are being transformed so radically.'

Chapter 5

1 'Europe – the Future', paper circulated by Mrs Thatcher to EC Heads of Government for the Fontainebleau meeting of the European Council, June 1984. Also referred to in Chapter 11.
2 A view shared by those on the left of the Conservative Party. See, in

particular, Michael Heseltine, *The Challenge of Europe: Can Britain Win?* (Weidenfeld and Nicolson, London, 1989).

3 See Peter Montagnon (ed.), *European Competition Policy* (RIIA/Pinter, London, 1990).

4 A study for the Department of Trade and Industry that was carried out by Coopers and Lybrand, *Barriers to Takeovers in the European Communities* (HMSO, London, December 1989), showed that British companies were the target in all but three of the 28 hostile bids made in the EC in 1988.

5 Michael Shackleton, *Financing the European Community* (RIIA/Pinter, London, 1990).

6 The British joined the Americans in strongly criticizing the proposal, but were somewhat inhibited because it was closely modelled on recently adopted UK legislation.

7 For a discussion of monetary compensatory amounts, see Michael Franklin, *Rich Man's Farming* (RIIA/Routledge, London, 1988), pp. 32–3, 62–4.

8 Article 13, Single European Act, *Official Journal of the European Communities*, no. L 169, 29 June 1987.

9 A quotation from Alan Butt Philip, *European Border Controls: Who Needs Them?*, Discussion Paper 19 (RIIA, London, 1989), p. 27. This is a useful background paper to the whole subject.

10 Ibid.

11 N. Colchester and D. Buchan, *Europe Relaunched: Truths and Illusions on the Way to 1992* (Hutchinson, London, 1990). A good example of this tendency lies in the collection of VAT. In its search for a frontier-free Europe, the Commission proposed a system which would treat intra-Community trade as if it were trade within a single country. This was universally opposed by the national administrations. The alternative (said by the Commission to be only temporary), whereby the collection of VAT will be on the basis of invoicing, may in the end prove to be more cumbersome than the system at the border which it replaces.

12 The Community in Education and Training for Technology (COMETT) scheme was adopted in 1985 and extended in 1989. The European Community Action Scheme for the Mobility of University Students (ERASMUS) was introduced in May 1987 and it, too, has been extended.

13 Late in his life, Jean Monnet said: 'If I could do it all again I would start with education'. Quoted by Michael Heseltine, *The Challenge of Europe*, who devotes a chapter to education.

14 See, for example, *Education and European Competence* (European Round Table of Industrialists, Brussels, January 1989).

15 In December 1989 the EC signed a new trade and aid Convention (Lomé

IV) with the African, Caribbean and Pacific (ACP) countries; this lasts for ten years but will be reviewed after five. Now that countries like Haiti and the Dominican Republic have joined the ACP countries, the rationale for this form of differentiation in favour of developing countries may come under review.

Chapter 6

1 EC Committee for the Study of Economic and Monetary Union (chaired by Jacques Delors), *Report on Economic and Monetary Union in the European Community*, Luxembourg, 12 April 1989.

2 *The European Communities. Text of the Communiqué issued by the Heads of State or of Government of the countries of the enlarged Community at their meeting in Paris on the 19th and 20th October 1972*, HMSO, London, Cmnd 5109.

3 *Membership of the European Community. Report on Renegotiation*, March 1975, HMSO, London, Cmnd 6003.

4 Writing in the *Royal Bank of Scotland Review*, June 1988, on 'Britain in Europe: left behind again?', Roy Jenkins said: 'Within six months of each other, Mr Callaghan and Mrs Thatcher told me . . . why each had stayed out [of the ERM]. Mr Callaghan said it was because he was afraid of being locked in at too high a rate which would prevent his dealing with unemployment. Mrs Thatcher said it was because she was afraid of being locked in at too low a rate which would prevent her dealing with inflation.'

5 *An Evolutionary Approach to Economic and Monetary Union*, HM Treasury, November 1989.

6 These proposals originated in a paper presented to the government in March 1990 by the Europe Committee of the British Invisible Exports Council (BIEC).

7 *European Monetary Union: a Business Perspective*, Confederation of British Industry, November 1989.

8 David G. Mayes, 'The Economic Impact of Monetary Union', paper prepared for the Conference on Monetary Union organized by the Federal Trust, London, 24 May 1990.

9 See, for example, DeAnne Julius, *Global Companies and Public Policy: the Growing Challenge of Foreign Direct Investment* (RIIA/Pinter, London, 1990), p. 12.

10 Mayes, op. cit.

11 *Britain and the European Communities: an Economic Assessment*, February 1970, HMSO, London, Cmnd 4289.

12 For example, by John Eatwell in a paper prepared for this study.

13 Discussed more fully in Chapter 7.

14 Karl Otto Pöhl, President of the German Bundesbank, in a lecture delivered in Paris, reported in *The Financial Times*, 17 January 1990.

15 See, for example, G. Davis, D. Currie, N. MacKinnon and I. Brinskill, '*Economic and Monetary Union: The Issues*', Institute for Public Policy Research, 1990. In 1989, the public-sector borrowing/lending requirement in the EC ranged from a net deficit equivalent to 20% of GNP in Greece to a surplus of 1.5% of GNP in the UK.

16 *A Strategy for the Ecu*, report prepared for the AMUE by Ernst and Young and the National Institute for Economic and Social Research, 1990.

17 Mayes, op. cit.

18 Sir Leon Brittan addressing the Federal Trust Conference on Monetary Union, London, 24 May 1990.

19 'My feeling is that the choice is between a single currency and a dominant currency', Mme Christiane Scrivener, EC Commissioner, speaking at a conference at Chatham House, London, 6 July 1990.

Chapter 7

1 See Michael Shackleton, *Financing the European Community* (RIIA/ Pinter, London, 1990), p. 13.

2 Ibid., Chapter 6.

3 *The Role of Public Finance in European Integration*, Vols I and II, Commission of the EC, Brussels, April 1977.

4 Tomaso Padoa-Schioppa et al., *Efficiency, Stability and Equity: A Strategy for the Evolution of the Economic System of the European Community*, Report of a Study Group appointed by the EC Commission (OUP, Oxford, 1987).

5 The Centre for Economic Policy Research has done some relevant work. See, for example, C. Bliss and J Braga de Macedo (eds.), *Unity with Diversity in the European Economy: The Community's Southern Frontier* (CEPR/CUP, Cambridge, 1990).

6 The standard work on the development of social policy is by Chris Brewster and Paul Teague: *European Community Social Policy: Its Impact on the UK* (Institute of Personnel Management, London, 1989).

7 *European Industrial Relations Review*, 192, January 1990, p. 13. Quoted by Dr Ann Robinson, Institute of Directors, in a paper for this study.

8 See, for example, the statement by the Confederation of British Industry, *A Europe of Opportunity for All*, September 1989.

9 Paper prepared for this study by Bill Jordan, Chairman, TUC Europe Committee.

10 UNICE Statement on the Social Charter, 19 October 1989.

11 Bill Jordan, op. cit.

12 For example, the TUC has expressed concern about the treatment of

black British citizens working in other member states without legal protection against racial discrimination (General Council Statement to the 1990 Trades Union Congress).

13 'The British Government has no doubt that there must be a social dimension in the Single European Market. But . . . that social dimension should be concerned above all with the creation of jobs', Rt Hon. Michael Howard, Secretary of State for Employment, in a speech on 29 June 1990.

Chapter 8

1 *Our Common Future*, Report of the World Commission on the Environment and Development (OUP, Oxford, 1987). This international Commission was chaired by Gro Brundtland, Prime Minister of Norway.

2 Indeed, it is conceivable that Community policies which have not prospered might in the future find themselves environmentally driven. The common energy policy is the most obvious example.

3 'The Community shall take action relating to the environment to the extent to which the objectives . . . can be attained better at Community level than at the level of the individual member states', Article 130R, paragraph 4.

4 Nigel Haigh and David Baldock, *Environmental Policy and 1992* (Institute for European Environmental Policy, London, 1989), p. 24.

5 Michael Heseltine, *The Challenge of Europe: Can Britain Win?* (Weidenfeld and Nicolson, London, 1989).

6 Paper prepared for this study by A.J. Fairclough, former Acting Director General, DG XI, EC Commission.

7 The Dutch proposal for a European Energy Agency, embracing both Western and Eastern Europe, falls into this category. A European agency similar to the European Environmental Agency but advising and perhaps adjudicating on mergers has also been suggested.

Chapter 9

1 Ernst Wistrich, *After 1992: the United States of Europe* (Routledge, London, 1989).

2 Paper presented by David Marquand for this study.

3 And always has done. Writing in his autobiography about the immediate postwar period, Denis Healey notes: 'We British . . . tended to regard a juridical commitment as defining the minimum you guarantee to fulfil. The Continentals tended to see it as setting an objective at which you aim

although you may fail to achieve it. Much of the tedious argument about federalism which divided us when we discussed the path to European unity was unnecessary once this was understood.' Denis Healey, *The Time of My Life* (Michael Joseph, London, 1989).

4 David Marquand, op. cit.

5 Resolution on the Intergovernmental Conference in the context of European Union (The Martin Report), adopted by the European Parliament on 12 July 1990 by 204 votes to 26 with 4 abstentions.

6 Report of the House of Commons Select Committee on Procedure, *The Scrutiny of European Legislation*, Vol. I, 8 November 1989.

7 Reported in *The Economist*, 7 July 1990.

8 Second Report of the Foreign Affairs Committee, *The Operation of the SEA*, House of Commons, Session 1989–90 (London, HMSO, May 1990), p. 6.

9 Critics of the powers of the Commission would rather see those powers taken away (which is not acceptable to most of the Community and would in any case make it unworkable) than give them greater legitimacy by having them democratically elected.

10 It is significant that when France challenged the Commission's right to use Article 90 to enhance its ability to deregulate the market in telecommunications, the British government decided not to associate itself with the challenge.

11 Peter Montagnon (ed.), *European Competition Policy* (RIIA/Pinter, London, 1990).

12 For an overview, see Marc Wilke and Helen Wallace, *Subsidiarity: Approaches to Power-sharing in the European Community* (RIIA Discussion Paper 27, London, 1990).

13 For instance, much media attention was given to a paper by the Institute of Directors in May 1990 entitled *European Union: a Business Leaders' View*, which argued that the concept of subsidiarity belonged only to a highly centralized, indeed unitary Europe and not to any form of federal structure. But in fact the concept is applicable in both cases and is certainly under discussion in the EC at present solely in relation to further stages in a long-running federal process.

14 House of Commons, *The Operation of the SEA*.

15 Article by the Foreign and Commonwealth Secretary, Rt Hon. Douglas Hurd, in *Le Monde*, 23 June 1990.

Chapter 10

1 This chapter draws heavily on the proceedings of a conference organized by the Royal Institute of International Affairs at Chatham House on 6 July 1990 and devoted entirely to hearing non-British views on the future development of the EC.

2 Speech by Dr Irmgard Adam-Schwätzer, Minister of State at the Federal Foreign Office of the FRG, at Chatham House, 6 July 1990.
3 'French foresee a homebound future in united Europe', in *The Guardian*, 3 January 1990.
4 Speech by Pedro Solbes, Spanish Secretary of State for the European Community, at Chatham House, 6 July 1990.
5 Uffe Elleman-Jensen, Danish Minister for Foreign Affairs, in a speech at Chatham House, 19 February 1990.
6 Speech by Klaus Jacobi, State Secretary at the Federal Department of Foreign Affairs of Switzerland, at Chatham House, 6 July 1990.
7 It is, for example, hardly surprising that the European Parliament so often takes a different view from the present British government when, following the 1989 elections, the Socialist Group secured a majority – thanks in large part to a big increase in the number of British Labour MEPs!

Chapter 11

1 A sentiment expressed by David Edwards in his book *Christians in a New Europe* (Collins, London, 1990): 'Since Germany cannot be locked up, it must be locked into a Europe at peace; and almost everything in the German record since the 1950s encourages the hope that this comfortable and dignified future will be welcomed.'
2 A phrase first used of the EC by Andrew Shonfield and taken by Christopher Tugendhat as the title for the final chapter of his book *Making Sense of Europe* (Viking, London, 1986).
3 As, for example, in Alan Sked, *A Proposal for European Union*, Bruges Group Occasional Paper 9, London, May 1990.
4 Christopher Tugendhat and William Wallace, *Options for British Foreign Policy in the 1990s* (RIIA/Routledge, London, 1988), p. 115.
5 Sir Leon Brittan makes both points in his Granada lecture 'Europe: Our Sort of Community', November 1989.
6 Ibid.
7 The problem has been that, when the Community has been reluctant to adopt British policy, the government has tended to fall back on the argument that the policy area in question should not be dealt with at the Community level. The French are not immune to the same tactics. Where a policy already exists, like the CAP, British criticism has often been vindicated by events but not well received at the time.
8 Reproduced in *Journal of Common Market Studies*, vol. 23 (1984), no. 1, p. 73.
9 The concluding paragraph reads: 'The progress that has been made towards "an ever-closer union of the peoples of Europe" of which the

Treaty of Rome speaks . . . is unlikely to be reversed. The objectives now must be:

– strengthen democracy and reinforce political stability in Europe . . .;

– develop a dynamic society in which industry thrives and activities which create wealth are encouraged . . .;

– strengthen the European pillar of the Alliance and the contribution Europe makes to its own security;

– promote policies which will improve the quality as well as the standard of life of the Community;

– with due regard for the needs of economic and industrial efficiency, do more to promote the improvement and the protection of the environment;

– agree urgently on certain organisational changes [spelt out in the paper];

– adopt policies which will guarantee the relevance of the Community to the problems, particularly unemployment, which affect our societies;

– take the necessary steps to strengthen the voice of the Community and make its influence felt in the world;

– heighten the consciousness among our citizens of what unites us.'

10 Tugendhat, *Making Sense of Europe.*

Also in this series

Financing the European Community
Michael Shackleton

This paper examines the implications of important innovations made by the February 1988 Delors package and subsequent institutional decisions for the future financing of the EC. '... explains a complex subject clearly and concisely' – *European Access.*

Published March 1990

The Transformation of Western Europe
William Wallace

This study looks at the interaction of political, security, economic and social developments since the European Communities were founded, notes the magnetic attraction of an integrating Europe for a widening circle of countries, and draws conclusions from these past trends for Europe's likely future development.

Published April 1990

The New Eastern Europe: Western Responses
J. M. C. Rollo

'... readable, up-to-date, relevant and concise ... once again Chatham House's team of experts has produced the right briefing at the right time' – George Robertson MP, *The House Magazine* (weekly journal of the Houses of Parliament)

Published April 1990

European Competition Policy
edited by Peter Montagnon

'... a very timely look at an area of Community politics that is at the heart of the 1992 programme and the future development of the European economy. Peter Montagnon tackles the subject with precision and authority, and achieves the difficult task of writing a book that makes sense to the layman while retaining credibility with the specialist.' – Giles Merritt, *The Financial Times.*

Published September 1990

RIIA/PINTER PUBLISHERS